The Euro-Arab Dialogue

The Euro-Arab Dialogue

A Study in Associative Diplomacy

Saleh A. Al-Mani'

Edited by
Salah Al-Shaikhly

Frances Pinter (Publishers), London

352779

327.405b ALM

821342.

Typeset by Joshua Associates, Oxford
Printed by SRP Ltd., Exeter

CONTENTS

LIST OF TABLES

LIST OF FIGURES

ABBREVIATIONS

ABEDA	Arab Bank for Economic Development in Africa
ACP Countries	Countries of Africa, the Caribbean, and the Pacific
CAP	Common Agricultural Policy (of the EC)
DAC	Development Assistance Committee (of the OECD)
EAD	Euro–Arab Dialogue
EC	European Community
EDF	European Development Fund (of the EC)
EIB	European Investment Bank (of the EC)
EPCS	European Political Co-operation System
EUA	European Units of Account
GATT	General Agreements on Tariffs and Trade
GSP	Generalized Scheme of Preferences (of the EC)
IBRD	International Bank for Reconstruction and Development
IDA	International Development Association
IEA	International Energy Administration
KFAED	Kuwaiti Fund for Arab Economic Development
LDC	Less developed country
NATO	North Atlantic Treaty Organization
OAPEC	Organization of Arab Petroleum Exporting Countries
OECD	Organization for Economic Co-operation and Development
OPEC	Organization of Petroleum Exporting Countries
PLO	Palestine Liberation Organization
UAE	United Arab Emirates
UN	United Nations
US	United States
USSR	Union of Soviet Socialist Republics

PREFACE

This book aims to give a general overview of the European Community's relations with the Arab World since 1973. It is based on my doctoral dissertation at the University of Southern California. In October 1981, the author had the privilege of presenting a summary paper to the Pio Manzu (International Research Centre on the Habitat) Conference held in Rimini, Italy, on the theme: 'The World Challenge: Europe/Arab Nation/Japan'. On the same panel Professor Al-Shaikhly submitted a research paper on the problems of the Euro–Arab dialogue and means for its revival.

Further discussions and collaboration with Dr Al-Shaikhly brought forth the realization of this book. He has kindly agreed to edit the book and issue it as part of the Centre for Research on the New International Economic Order series on North–South relations.

The author is indebted to Dr Al-Shaikhly for his contribution and refinement of the original manuscript. His sage criticism and continous encouragement and dedication up to the final stages of publication is warmly acknowledged. Special thanks is due to my doctoral committee at USC and my thesis editor, Marje Cappellari. Needless to say, I alone bear the responsibility for any shortcomings.

SALEH A. AL–MANI'
Riyadh
1983

Dr Saleh A. Al-Mani' is currently an Assistant Professor of Political Science at King Saud University in Riyadh, Saudi Arabia. He earned his Ph.D. in International Relations from the University of Southern California in 1981, and had taught at King Abdul-Aziz University.

PART I

INTRODUCTION

1 THE EURO-ARAB DIALOGUE: AN OVERVIEW

Like any other initiative, the Euro-Arab Dialogue (EAD) had its supporters and sceptics. When the idea was first put forward, immediately after the Arab–Israeli war of October 1973, it had many supporters and even the sceptics were willing to give it a try. However, as the dialogue progressed, without producing any tangible results, even the most ardent supporters began to doubt the seriousness of the European intentions. The sceptics were being proved right.

In this chapter a brief summary is presented of the process of the dialogue, while the rest of the book is devoted to a more scientific and comprehensive approach to the notion of the EAD as an exercise in associative diplomacy.

The Arab–Israeli war of October 1973 had a direct influence on the European initiative. There was the immediate threat of an oil embargo, a wider support internationally for the Arab point of view in the Middle East conflict, and a relatively unified Arab position. Most important of all, however, the Europeans were expecting—and rightly so—a sudden influx of wealth into the region.

An initial contact was made between the two sides in June 1974 and the first meeting was held at the headquarters of the League of Arab States in Cairo. On 31 July 1974 another meeting was held in Paris, where a number of organizational issues were settled. On 20 October 1974 a second meeting was held in Cairo at the 'expert' level to discuss and settle the details of the first meeting of the General Committee, scheduled to be held in Paris on 26 Octobr 1974. This meeting did not take place, as a new and rather thorny political question was introduced into the discussions, the question of the representation of the Palestine Liberation Organization (PLO) in the Arab delegation to the dialogue. The problem was technically solved, however, after the European side proposed that delegates to the negotiations could be on a regional rather than a national basis. Thus there would be a 'European delegation' and an 'Arab delegation', without any reference to the nationalities of the individual members of each side. In 1975 two meetings took place, one in Rome and the other in Abu Dhabi. The meeting in Abu Dhabi—which was convened in November 1975—decided to form a working group to deal with the questions relating to financial and investment institutions.

The General Committee of the EAD, however, did not meet until May 1976 in Luxembourg and only at the level of ambassadors, not at the level of foreign ministers as was previously envisaged. A wide range of issues was discussed at this meeting, including finance, trade, industry, agriculture, and science and technology.

The Arab side was anxious that some form of understanding should be reached on guarantees of the value of investments and other Arab assets held in Europe. The Arabs even indicated during the discussions that some form of agreement would be desirable in this respect. The European side, however, felt that no guarantee could be given on the value of Arab investments because it was subject to the rates of inflation that Europe expected, and would experience, in the future. The Europeans felt that inflation was a world-wide phenomena and that they could not give any guarantees against it. On the other hand, the Europeans suggested that the preparation of a guideline on investment opportunities and investment guarantee loans, in both the Arab and European regions, would be sufficient for this purpose. The proposals of agreements on science and technology put forward by the Arab side met with similar objections from the Europeans. It was only in the areas of trade and agricultural development that some form of consensus was reached. In fact, even this consensus was more of a rhetoric than a hard and tangible proposal.

Seven working committees were formed to deal with a number of economic activities. These were: industry, science and technology, infrastructure, financial co-operation, commerce, agricultural development, and labour, social, and cultural issues. The industry and infrastructure committees were further subdivided into five and three subcommittees respectively.

Some Observations on the Process of the EAD

Over eight years have now elapsed since the EAD first started. Very few attempts have been made so far to assess the organizational aspects of the various meetings.

Invitations to most committee meetings or expert group meetings were usually initiated by the European side, and it invariably proposed the date for such meetings. The League of Arab States was then informed and it in turn contacted each individual Arab government. At other times, the European side would contact the Arab envoys in Brussels and the envoys would then contact their respective countries. It is no exaggeration to say that, more often than not, the Arab side was taken by surprise as to the date and agenda of these meetings. Very little time was allocated for adequate preparation for them. Furthermore, the European side would ask for the names of the proposed Arab participants as well as for a list of proposals the Arab side wished to tackle during these meetings. The European side, however, seldom gave the names of its own participants in advance, nor did it list its own proposals. The co-ordination amongst the Arab group was rather weak and hasty; the only subcommittee that seems to have done its homework thoroughly was the science and technology subcommittee. Unfortunately, the European side seems to have thwarted every effort this subcommittee has made to reach a meaningful agreement on the question of transfer of technology.

In examining the minutes of the various committees and subcommittees, there seems to be very little in concrete terms about joint projects or useful schemes. The minutes often speak in terms of the demands of the Arab side or the demands of the European side, of resolutions and recommendations or studies to be prepared by one side or another, without any reference to a plan of action.

An Analysis of the European Approach to the EAD

During the first four years of the EAD the Europeans were very active, and their behaviour indicated that they were serious about bringing the initiative to a successful conclusion. As new economic and political factors evolved the European side began to lose interest, and there were fewer and fewer meetings.

During this period the European side gained a great deal on all fronts. The EAD managed to pacify a number of Arab countries in the hope that Europe would change its stand on the Palestinian issue. The security of the oil supply continued and the strategic reserves were at their highest. The financial surpluses were recycled through the European (and American) banking systems, and Europe's trade with the Arab region quadrupled in value. In other words, Europe managed to recover from the impact of the first 'oil shock' without compromising its traditional political and economic stands.

It is also interesting to note that throughout the EAD the European side insisted that political issues should be discussed separately from issues of economic co-operation. The European side resisted very strongly the formulation of a joint political committee along the lines of the other committees, which were 'economic' in nature. The joint communiqué issued after the meeting of the General Committee in Luxembourg stated that economic growth in the Arab and European regions would serve the best interests of both sides and was essential for a successful and continuous co-operation, and that no effort should be spared in achieving such an objective. The statement went on to explain that there should be a continuous exchange of views and ideas between the two sides on the current economic situation and future expectations.

The European argument for separating political issues from economic discussions was not very convincing. Its argument was contrary to previous European practice in dealing with many international, European, and national questions. European insistence on such a separation in the EAD was obviously to avoid any commitment on the Palestinian issue. What probably made things worse from the Arab point of view was that the Europeans continued to strengthen their economic, financial, and scientific ties with Israel. In 1975, the same European group which was conducting the dialogue with the Arabs signed an economic co-operation agreement with Israel. There were a number of concessions made to Israel in this agreement, whereby Israeli agricultural and manufactured products enjoyed favourable treatment in the European market.

The Arab efforts to gain similar agreements and concessions were frustrated. The Europeans refused to offer any preferential treatment in terms of trade to any non-Mediterranean

Arab country on the grounds that it was against the declared policies of the EC countries. The contradiction here, of course, is that the discussions between the two sides were taking place in the context of the EAD and that the whole purpose of the dialogue was to overcome any previous policies and restrictions which had been declared regarding the Arab region as a whole.

The other contradiction during the process of the EAD was in the area of science and technology. The Europeans did not find it possible to conclude an agreement on transfer of technology with the Arab side. A number of explanations were offered by the European side. The Europeans suggested, for example, that this issue should be referred to the global negotiations which were taking place in the UN, or to higher policy-making institutions in each region. On other occasions, the Europeans insisted that as the private sector controlled technology the governments could not enter into agreements in that area. They therefore proposed that the issue be discussed on a project by project basis. As a free-market economy, the Europeans could have offered the same excuse at every point, since the private sector also controls finance, banking, trade, industry, etc. As it turned out, this was another European tactic to block any meaningful conclusion to the EAD.

The Arab Approach to the EAD

Twenty-one Arab countries, under the auspices of the League of Arab States, took part in the EAD. Although there were serious efforts to prepare and co-ordinate unified positions, the Arab side did not pay much attention to certain vital details which were a background to the EAD. The Arab side, for example, was not fully conversant with European mentality, patterns of behaviour, or negotiating strategy. The Arab side was not clear about the final European objective, and in some instances it was not too clear about its own objectives. The Arab side also failed to recognize the real influence of the United States on the European approach to the EAD. On a number of occasions the American influence was clearly felt on both sides, especially on the question of energy or the political issue of the Palestinian participation in the EAD.

At certain points of the dialogue the Arab position was rather weak, lacking a unified position, joint strategy, and the collective bargaining power that the European side enjoyed. The different interest groups within the Arab side seem to have given the Europeans sufficient reason to come up with such notions as the European–Gulf dialogue or the European–North African dialogue. Arab negotiators do not seem to have considered any fallback positions. They could, for example, have initiated or hinted at a parallel dialogue with other economic groups in Africa, Asia, Latin America or even the Socialist bloc or Japan. The idea of such a tactic would be to demonstrate to the Europeans that other alternatives were available to the Arab side should the EAD fail, and to widen the political base or diversify sources of trade, technology, and other material development inputs.

Assuming also that the Arab side was serious about obtaining some political or economic concessions from the Europeans, it does not seem to have applied any pressure to gain these concessions. During the period 1974–9 the Arab oil producers were supplying most of Europe's energy needs. The Europeans would have conceded a lot of ground to the Arab negotiators had the Arabs hinted at the use of the 'oil weapon'. The security of the supply of energy was of utmost importance to the Europeans during this period, especially while there were a number of uncertainties in the Gulf region. The other pressure point which the Arabs could have used was that of their financial surpluses and investments held in Europe. The Western financial institutions and money markets being what they are (that is, very sensitive to speculations) a mere announcement or statement of a controversial nature would have made the Europeans rethink their tactics in the EAD.

Summary of Conclusions

From the outset, even at the early stages like the Cairo meeting and the meetings in Rome and Abu Dhabi, there were noted differences between the points of view of Europe and the Arab countries. The Europeans, for example, envisaged the whole dialogue as basically economic with some political overtones attached to it, while the Arab side viewed the EAD as a political and economic dialogue. The Arabs were hoping that both these concepts would go side by side, and that they would not go ahead with the economic dialogue without securing some political gains.

In all fairness to the participants in this dialogue, it was a very complicated one in the sense that it involved some thirty countries from both sides and had on its agenda some of the most complicated economic and political issues of the past thirty years. Even if everyone had been serious and sincere about the EAD, it would not have taken any less time or encountered any less difficulties than it did. For the first three years of the EAD both sides were trying to explore the other's points of view in the hope that after this stage there would be a meaningful content to the whole idea of the EAD. Unfortunately, the basic reasons which brought the European initiative for this dialogue began to subside, and gradually the European side felt less and less motivated to continue with it. The collective European position toward the political dimension of the EAD was, and still remains, less progressive than the positions of certain individual European countries. In other words, at a time when individual countries were looking at the Palestinian issue with some sympathy, the EC as a whole maintained its objections to PLO participation *per se*. This had more serious consequences during the meetings of the General Committee. So much time was devoted to discussions of this political issue that very little time was spent on substantive economic discussions.

The Arab League, for its part, could at best only act as a co-ordinator. Under the provisos of its present charter it has no powers of endorsement on behalf of individal countries, and no authority to enforce or implement a resolution affecting individual Arab countries. The Arab League will be in a much stronger position if its proposed new charter is endorsed and it is given a clear mandate on the issues under discussion.

Finally, the Arab side must evaluate this experience objectively and thoroughly to see if there are any lessons that can be learned about the negotiating capabilities of the Arab countries, about their ability to put forward effective ideas and unified points of view and to make use of all the tools that modern political science can provide.

2 CONCEPTS OF DEPENDENCE

The study of interdependence—'the ability of a state to influence and to be influenced by the policy of another state over a period of time within the same policy sector'—found its way into the social sciences through the efforts of economists to explain disturbances in the late 1960s in the balance of payments between the United States and Europe. In 1968, Richard Cooper[1] called to the attention of economic policy makers the growing economic interdependence of Western nations and advocated the internationalization of US economic and monetary policies.

As students of international politics began to address normatively economic issues in American foreign policy, the term 'interdependence' began to enjoy a certain vogue in both academic writing and in policy makers' pronouncements. Both forums heralded the onset of a new era in international relations in which states could no longer enjoy the autonomy or quasi-autonomy possible in the past. Small states, and even 'medium powers', have always been aware of this. Now it was believed that even major powers could no longer enjoy relative autarky and remain isolated from currents of change in international economic relations.

Robert Keohane and Joseph Nye and their associates began in the mid-1970s to speak of the 'interconnectedness' of states. At the beginning their work was an attempt to defend the phenomenon of the multinational corporation as a vehicle for global efficiency and growth. However, later writings extended to include a wide range of policies, issues, and patterns of negotiations in economic and monetary regimes, such as those in US–Canadian and US–Australian relations.[2] Students of European integration, largely the adherents of Ernst B. Haas, also set out to revise their neofunctionalist paradigm and seized upon the concept of interdependence to explain what seemed at the time to be the disarray of the European Community under external pressures.[3]

In order to explain many political associations, convenient definitions were now being given of the word interdependence. Some defined it as 'mutual dependence', or 'the quality or state of being influenced, conditional upon, or necessitated by something else, or approval of others'.[4] Mutual dependence does not require absolute or equal dependence, since the issues involved might not be equal in intensity, nor are they easily interchanged or traded. Issues perceived by one nation as urgent may not necessarily be perceived as equally urgent by another. Hence, the ability of a state or group of states to direct the attention of other states to its own priorities depends upon the ability to influence and on the solidity of the ties that bind one group to another. One aspect of interdependence is power and the ability to influence relations. Another aspect is the characteristics of specific structures of dependence. Therefore, interdependence is multifaceted and its definition is syncretic.

Keohane and Nye have viewed interdependence in terms of 'policy interdependence' or the extent to which decisions taken by actors in one part of a system affect (intentionally or unintentionally) other actors' policy decisions elsewhere in the system.[5] They differentiate between 'policy interdependence' and 'policy integration' (the ability to co-ordinate policies of different international actors to minimize unintended conflict arising from the adoption of non-congruent policies). In a refinement of their earlier model, Keohane and Nye linked the two concepts of power and interdependence to make the latter conditional upon the former. Interdependence was explained in terms of the two dimensions, 'sensitivity' and 'vulnerability'. Sensitivity relates to degrees of responsiveness 'of one policymaker to policies pursued by other decision-makers in other polities'. Vulnerability interdependence is of a higher order and refers to the 'costliness' of alternative policies.[6]

The vulnerability of a state is said to condition 'regime changes' in the political processes and negotiations among them, while structural changes do not necessarily occur except through political/military upheavals, such as major wars. However, regimes may also change through the persistent demands of the least advantaged partner(s) in dependent relations. The pressure brought about by Third World countries on the one hand, and French pressures in the 1970s on the other, are said to have been the driving force behind the modest changes in the international monetary regime.

In studying the American–European frames of monetary interdependence, Edward Morse linked the concept to that of 'crisis diplomacy'. He argued that competitive monetary policies in the US and France led to a series of 'crises of adjustments', said to be a natural outcome of 'specified actions taken by two or more parties, when such actions are mutually contingent'. Interdependence, then, for Morse is both a *condition* and a *perception*, though the latter, or conscious perception of inter-dependent behaviour, is said to be necessary for the manipulation of interdependent relations.[7]

Interdependence can also be manifested in the security realm of inter-state relations. Richard Gunther has defined strategic interdependence as a perception of fear in which 'a state system fears that the rules of the exchange or transaction might be changed by the other system, hence its military policies reflect such fear'. Gunther devised a formula by which to approximate vulnerability interdependence in terms of intra-block military expenditures.[8]

Harold Jacobson has also defined interdependence in terms of vulnerability and policy interdependence. He emphasized that the current involvement of states in webs or networks of international organizations is an indication that the West-phalian system of sovereign states is no longer viable in today's international system. Accordingly, international organizations are said to be 'vehicles for dispersion of a state's political authority' and can be best seen as communication channels for co-ordinating incongruent actions.[9]

From the foregoing discussion, it is apparent that the notion of interdependence is a summary concept best defined as relational intrusiveness (namely Keohane's 'vulnerability' and Morse's 'condition'), a manipulative phenomenon in which the perception of actions and interests necessitates some kind of reactive or manipulative behaviour. Keohane and others have argued that interdependent behaviour occurs in a given system. They have failed to recognize that interdependence may be a *result* of structural changes. The United Nations was conceived during the Second World War primarily to regulate an impending post-war strategic interdependence between the US and the USSR. Similarly, the Euro–Arab Dialogue and the concomitant intra-block associative diplomacy were created as a means of regularizing, controlling, and even manipulating the emerging system of Euro–Arab interdependence, especially after October 1973.

The relational aspect of interdependence leads the analyst to cast the definition of interdependence in a new light. One can no longer speak of 'mutual dependence' or reciprocal influence, except in terms of specific policy sectors. One can say, for example, that the US and the Soviet Union are militarily or strategically interdependent, but not necessarily economically interdependent. One can also speak of European–American interdependence in monetary affairs, or perhaps of American–British interdependence in foreign policy. Thus, our analysis of interdependent relations among states or systems of states is viewed within a certain policy sector and cannot be applied indiscriminately to all policy sectors.

Just as one speaks of monetary interdependence, it is clearly plausible to speak of trade dependence, energy dependence, or financial dependence. One can also speak of mutual dependence that does not add up to interdependence, except within the scope of a single sector. Mutual dependence is therefore not a sufficient description of interdependence, and the original definition must be rewritten for a new condition. As a result, interdependence could be viewed as mutual and reciprocal dependence within the same parameters of a specified policy sector.

Additionally, a nation state may attempt to manipulate and control its interdependent relations with other states, depending upon their differing national or regional attributes of power. Their initial dependence on the outside world testifies to their inability as a nation or a group of nations to pursue their national goals autonomously. That is, interdependence dictates by definition lack of autonomy. Just as foreign input is needed for proper functioning of the system, be it an economy or a polity, foreign interference must be accepted and/or resisted according to the distribution of elements of national and bureaucratic power. Hence, in a national setting, states would continuously adjust their foreign policy according to the conditions and relations of interdependence with other states in their environment.

To assert that a foreign-policy maker can adjust the foreign policy of his nation according to conditions of interdependence is an ideal, liberal interpretation that may not always apply to small or developing countries whose colonial and political/ economic legacy may continue to bind them to the wheels of their former masters. Those countries may have attained formal political independence, but their trade patterns may still exhibit some form of structural dependence. For example, Algerian agricultural trade with the European Community (EC), especially France, is dependent to some extent on the export of wine, a colonial product which is geared to a foreign market and which, by virtue of religion and tradition, could not be consumed in appreciable amounts in the local market. The ability of Algeria to sell its wine on the French market has been dependent to some extent on the ebb and flow of French–Algerian political relations.

Can one, then, view Algerian trade with France and the EC in terms of dependent relations, or in terms of mutual interdependence? After all, France and the EC are equally dependent on Algerian supplies of hydrocarbons, especially natural gas, and such a relation could conceivably be viewed as a form of interdependence. Since both dependence and interdependence are a continuum of one another and can only be distinguished in extreme cases, the objectivity of the analyst is of primary consideration here.

Dependencia and Interdependence

Interdependence has been previously defined as mutual, though not necessarily symmetrical, dependence. *Dependencia*, on the other hand, can be defined as exclusivism, or one-sided influence. Theotonio Dos Santos, one of the fathers of *dependencia*, has defined it as a 'situation in which the economy of certain countries is conditioned by the expansion of another economy to which the former is subjected'.[10]

As a theory of political economy, *dependencia* has its roots in studies of economic development models and their applicability to development in Brazil. Theorists in the field attempted to challenge the mainstream interpretation of economic development as an extension of development from one region to another and as a spillover of new techniques and modes of production from one sector of the economy to other, under-developed sectors.

André Gunder Frank argued that economic development in Latin American countries could only occur 'independently' of their exploitative and diffusive relations with the capitalist world economy. He further hypothesized that almost every spasm of 'self-generating' economic development in Latin America since the Spanish depression of the seventeenth century had occurred as a result of temporary isolation. The inter-war period and the depression of 1929 saw a 'loosening of trade and investment ties' which helped the cities of Sao Paulo in Brazil and Mendoza and Rosario in the interior of Argentina, and Paraguay, to experience a classical industrial development.[11]

Economic development, for proponents of the *dependencia* school, lies in autonomy and in reduced reliance on external trade, especially single-crop exports. It is argued that most of the bourgeoisie in underdeveloped countries derive their wealth not from production but from commercial transactions with the North. Even if the centres of trade in the South prosper, cities in the interior do not necessarily follow suit; in fact they may even suffer, since the accumulation of wealth in one geographical centre, which is said to be a structural element of the global extension of capitalism, tends to create a scarcity of wealth and manpower in the national hinterland.

Analogously, Johan Galtung has developed a political theory of dependency (or a structural theory of imperialism) in which the world is divided between a 'centre' and a 'periphery'. Political interaction of the centre of the periphery with the centre of the capitalist world is greater than with its own national periphery. Such a political interpretation is con-ditioned, if not governed, by a vision of economic exploitation in the dependent countries and in the unequal relations of the South to the North. It is an over-encompassing, neo-Marxist interpretation of international transactions and relations, or what this author calls the exclusivism principle, which sees sociological relations, whether at the world or national level, as merely meaningful in dualistic, zero-sum terms.[12]

From this discussion, we see a conflict of original precepts between the *dependencia* school and that of interdependence. The *dependencia* school is based on a cognition of exploitation and dominance, while interdependence addresses structures of collaboration based on a positivistic notion of man's relations with other men as largely co-operative. Interdependence is based on the liberal notion of pluralism, which sees political goods as a result of infighting among competing, equal groups, and sees these results as package deals and solutions that satisfy the interests of many, not exclusively those of a single group. The *dependencia* school also differs from interdependence in the choice of units of analysis. The interdependence school is largely based on the nation state and its bureaucratic groups. The distinction between the two schools is not merely theoretical, but political as well.

Proponents of interdependence, such as Ernst Haas, have attacked the *dependencia* theorists as advocates of a 'political doctrine' for the Southern poor, and asserted that their theory could not therefore be considered as 'knowledge', which has a universal acceptance.[13] In turn, *dependistas* have labelled Northern models and modalities of interdependence as largely 'empty and utopian'.[14]

The quandary which every analyst faces is the selection of the appropriate theory to apply to his research question. Most of the studies of interdependence analyse relations among advanced Western industrial countries, while those of *dependencia* address relations between industrial countries and their peripheries, such as US–Latin American relations.

The Euro–Arab Relationship

The choice of topic of this study—Euro–Arab relations— could, therefore, be viewed through the *dependencia* paradigm if one was concerned with sub-state units such as multinational corporations. However, since our concern is with the state and its international organizations, we cannot adopt the *dependencia* model and must search for other paradigms. Additionally, the *dependencia* model might be applicable to certain historical periods in which the dependence of one state on another is unidimensional and clear-cut, but it cannot be applied to the study of every period of interaction between the North and the South. While the Arab states may have been truly dependent on Europe in, say 1955, they could not be described as being equally and solely dependent on the EC countries and their markets in 1978. The argument here is that a body of theory is not a dictum which is valid for all states throughout history. It is a relational theory that is time-dependent. The Arab states might be said to have been dependent on Europe in the 1960s, but conceivably they could have achieved a state of mutual dependence during the 1970s and 1980s.

While colonial trade dependency remains relevant in some Arab countries, such as Morocco or the Sudan, or may have increased in Egypt, it has declined since 1974 for the oil-producing Arab states. Further, the expansion of internal Arab labour markets has not only provided new markets for surplus labour in densely populated countries, but has also provided new job opportunities for Europeans. Thus, one can convincingly argue that there has been effective interdependence between Europe and the Arab world in the labour market. However, it might be easier for a British engineer who has lost his job in Saudi Arabia to find a job in another EC country than for an unskilled Algerian labourer who has lost his job or work permit in France to find a new job in Kuwait. Therefore, if the Arab labour market is said to be interdependent with that of Europe it remains, none the less, an asymmetrical interdependence.

Since not all Arab economies are 'subsistence' economies, nor are most major productive industries in the Arab world owned by foreign enterprises (two of the criteria of the *dependencia* school), the Arab economies are not totally dependent on those of Western Europe. However, as we have pointed out, Algeria is totally dependent on French and other European markets for selling raw wine, and obviously the Europeans are largely dependent on Arab supplies of hydrocarbons. Does this amount to interdependence, since it is characterized by a mutuality of interests in maintaining levels of trade flow? Perhaps the answer lies in providing new alternative views of Euro–Arab dependence relations that cannot be explained in terms of zero-sum games, and which take into consideration the colonial structures of agricultural trade that bind the Mahgreb countries of Algeria, Morocco, and Tunisia to the EC markets.

James Caporaso has attempted to redefine the two contradictory concepts of dependence and interdependence in terms of a generalized notion of dependence. The two contradictory notions would thus be merely special cases within a larger phenomenon of dependence. Caporaso defines dependence as 'the pattern of external reliance of well-integrated nation-states on one another'.[15] Dependence is also said to be a function of 'the size of the reliance of relationships, importance of the good on which one relies, and case, availability, and cost of the replacement alternatives'.[16]

Caporaso linked the notion of dependence to that of power, asserting that power 'occupies a critical transition role'.[17] For Caporaso:

> There are two primary links between dependence and power. The first link is that structural asymmetries are basic for power, i.e., these asymmetries provide the resources to affect others by depriving them of the desired exchanged goods. . . . The second link is that dependence, quite apart from its consequences for manifest decisional power, is itself a form of value-allocating process . . . that is, the capabilities, structural positions, and asymmetric dependent relations are themselves capable of leading to certain distributions of values quite apart from the overt decisional process.[18]

In applying Caporaso's theory to the decision by the Nixon Administration in 1972 to withhold the sale of American wheat to Chile, one sees that the conditions of Chile's food dependence on the US went beyond the parameters of the decision itself to highlight the importance of that asymmetric relationship for the viability of Chilean polity *per se*. The Chilean leadership had to maintain the status quo or ultimately face not only the loss of American wheat but the demise of the polity as well. This extreme example illustrates the linkages of dependence relations to power, especially that of 'geo-economic' spheres of influence.

To cite another example, the ability of a small country like Tunisia to market its surplus olive oil in EC markets is dependent upon the continuation of European goodwill toward that country. A change of heart in Brussels might alter not only the direction of this trade but might also affect the future political leanings of the Tunisian leadership, i.e. away from Europe toward another power. A third example of the importance of Caporaso's two links can be found in the November 1973 decision of the Organization of Arab Petroleum Exporting Countries (OAPEC) to embargo sales of Arab crude oil to the Netherlands. This demonstrated that the Europeans could not be allowed to intervene (as was alleged) in the Arab–Israeli war without facing countermeasures.[19] The decision prompted the reformulation of previous dependent structures by introducing a new set of dependent relations, as well as by inserting a new, and in the Arab eyes more equitable, 'value-allocating process'.

In summary, Caporaso's definition of dependence, which will be adopted in this study, not only views dependence as a 'net reliance on others', but also indicates a certain distributional character of geo-economic influence. States and regional organizations do not merely exhibit a certain asymmetrical dependence on other states and regions, they have a vital stake in the maintenance of such structures of dependence, since these structures could be manipulated to enhance and/or decrease the power (i.e. influence) of some states at the expense of their partners in the dependent relations. The more unequal the asymmetries of a relationship, the higher the importance of the relationship for one of the two partners.

Regional Dependence: A New Class of Dependence Relations

Associative diplomacy was defined earlier as a form of simple interdependence in which regional organizations interact regularly to complement each other's lack of security in certain policy sectors. European associative diplomacy toward the Arab world can also be viewed from the perspective of a particular case of dependence, that of regional dependence.

Regional dependence is a certain class of dependence— exogenous reliance, structurally determined—which exhibits an unrequited transfer of resources. These resources could be monetary, political, or economic—tangible, or intangible (such as willingness to abide by the rules of the dependence regime). Regional dependence usually displays conditions for asymmetric interaction, but this term can also describe complementarities in which each side is aware of its lack of a certain product or service and is willing to acquire it in exchange for external support in another policy sector. One side may even be willing to enhance the bargaining by providing additional incentives, such as economic aid or other forms of support, without the expectation of reward. In other words, a state or system of states might be willing to extend a certain amount of unrequited transfer for the maintenance of a certain dependence, *ergo* regional dependence.

Foreign aid, in this context, should not be confused with foreign aid that is the result of normal diplomatic behaviour in bargaining and negotiations. The extension of unrequited transfers in negotiations is merely a single act that is expected to make an important deal more attractive at a specific period of time; the product of this may be so intangible as to be incalculable.

Attributes of Regional Dependence

Regional dependence has been defined as an economic function measured in terms of trade reliance (sensitivity), opportunity cost of that reliance (vulnerability), and the extension of aid or unrequited transfers of goods or resources to maintain the dynamics of an asymmetric exchange; that is, to maintain the conditions of dependence over a certain period of time. Regional dependence provides a substructure upon which other forms of negotiation and other regional structural organizations are based. It is a basis for the exertion and manifestation of power and inter-regional influence.

Aid, as part of the substructure, helps cement the organizational superstructure. A superpower which attempts to maintain a certain international order is expected to build international institutions to manage the underlying structures of dependence. Joint commissions are entrusted with the appropriation of the aid commitments of a major power to its dependent states. Systematic aid, therefore, tends to lubricate the wheels of dependence to ensure the requisite consensus of the élites of other states for the maintenance of a particular dependent relation.

Aid should not be viewed in this context as unidimensional or unidirectional. It is conceivable that two states could exchange, not necessarily equally, two types of aid. State A may be induced to sell a certain product to its partners in the dependent relation at a price lower than the going market price. Thus, the difference between the going world market price and the actual price received by State A from its partner is a form of unrequited transfer and can be viewed as indirect aid. After 1973, the oil-producing countries resorted to this form of 'dependent' relations in their oil trade with like-minded developing countries.

Regional dependence does not necessarily translate into symmetrical dependence within a particular policy/economic sector. Two states may exhibit mutual dependence (which has been defined earlier as not necessarily equal to conditions of interdependence), but they could not be described as interdependent unless that condition pertained to the same policy/economic sector. Further, the states may also extend differing types of aid and not necessarily be interdependent except in the same aid sector, say food aid, investment aid, or even foreign-policy support. When the European foreign ministers supported President Carter's economic sanctions against Iran in 1980, the ministers were providing a form of aid and support which was an expression of interest in the continuation of American–West European dependence relations.

Just as aid is not unidirectional, dependence relations are not necessarily a zero-sum game. Two states or systems of states could become benefactors of a certain dependence relation, but not by the same measure. A condition of regional dependence that must be satisfied is that the gains, whether strategic, political, diplomatic, or economic, are not equally distributed among the partners. Conversely, if a certain dependence relation can be identified, the direction of utmost gain in that relationship must be investigated, even if that gain is qualitative, as in the case of the creation of spheres of influence.

Inasmuch as it relates to North–South relations, associative diplomacy differs from the complex interdependence which describes dependence relations among advanced industrial countries.[20] Regional dependence is not restricted to a state-to-state relation or to the relations of regional organizations. Regional dependence lacks the bureaucratic interaction, or sub-state interaction as the case may be, that is evident in, say, American–Canadian relations. The preponderance of power in regional dependence is less acute than in North–North dependence, since the latter may tie the partners into a security arrangement, such as the North Atlantic Treaty Organization (NATO) or the Warsaw Pact, and to a lesser degree the Arab League.

Notes

1. See Cooper's earliest writing on this topic in R. Cooper, *The Economics of Interdependence: Economic Policy in the Atlantic Community* (New York, McGraw-Hill, 1968).
2. For the evolution of the thoughts of Keohane and Nye, see their three major writings: *Transnational Relations and World Politics* (Cambridge, Mass., Harvard University Press, 1971); their chapter, 'International Interdependence and Integration', in F. Greenstein and N. Polsby (eds), *Handbook of Political Science*, Vol. 8, *International Politics* (Reading, Mass., Addison-Wesley, 1975); and their more mature work, *Power and Interdependence, World Politics in Transition* (Boston, Little, Brown, and Co., 1977).
3. E. B. Haas, *The Obsolescence of Regional Integration Theory* (Research Series No. 25, University of California Institute of International Studies, 1975).
4. *Webster's Third New International Dictionary of the English Language* (1961).
5. Keohane and Nye, 'International Interdependence and Integration', in Greenstein and Polsby (eds), op. cit., pp. 11–13.
6. Ibid.
7. E. Morse, 'Crisis Diplomacy, Interdependence, and the Politics of International Economic Relations', in R. Tanter and R. Ullman (eds), *Theory and Policy in International Relations* (Princeton, Princeton University Press, 1972), p. 133.
8. For Gunther block military penetration equals the percentage of block military expenditures. See his work which appears as Appendix II, 'Block GNP—Indicators of Economic and Military Interdependence', in Haas, op. cit., pp. 103-5.
9. H. K. Jacobson, *Networks of Interdependence: International Organizations and the Global Political System* (New York, Alfred Knopf, 1979), p. 7.
10. T. Dos Santos, 'The Structure of Interdependence', *American Economic Review, Papers and Proceedings* 60 (May 1970), p. 231.
11. A. Gunder Frank, 'The Development of Underdevelopment', in R. Rhodes (ed.), *Imperialism and Underdevelopment, A Reader* (New York, Monthly Review Press, 1970), pp. 10-11.
12. J. Galtung, 'A Structural Theory of Imperialism', *Journal of Peace Research*, 2 (1971), 81-118.
13. See Haas's recent article, 'Why Collaborate? Issue-Linkages and International Regimes', *World Politics*, 32 (April 1980), 357-405, p. 370.
14. Dos Santos, op. cit., p. 236.
15. See the edited issue of *International Organization*, 30 (Winter 1978), especially James Caporaso's article on 'Dependence, Dependency and Power in the Global System', 13-42.

16. Ibid., p. 13.
17. Ibid., p. 28.
18. Ibid., pp. 28-9.
19. It has been argued that the embargo resulted from an earlier embargo of arms sales to the Arab states by European suppliers, as well as because of an alleged shipment of trucks from the Netherlands to support the Israeli war effort.
20. For a full discussion of North-North interdependence relations, see Keohane and Nye, *Power and Interdependence, World Politics in Transition*, cited in Note 2.

3 THE REGIONAL DEPENDENCE OF THE EUROPEAN COMMUNITY ON THE ARAB WORLD

Introduction

In this chapter, the concept of regional dependence is re-examined, and a set of governing conditions is introduced for the analysis of this type of dependence. The theory is also advanced that Euro–Arab regional dependence has tended to encourage the adoption, as a starting point, of a policy of linkage with the Arab region on the part of the European Community (EC) through the instrument of aid.

The Arab states, members of the League of Arab States, constitute an international region, since a portion of their foreign economic and political policies are expressed through regional organizations such as the League of Arab States and its specialized agencies. For Western European countries, the EC epitomizes the definition of a regional organization. The EC is, theoretically, in virtual control of European foreign trade policies, and it is increasingly extending its activities into new spheres with the goal of harmonizing the economic and political policies of its member European countries.

International regional dependence differs from internal regional dependence in that the latter merely reflects adjustments of various policies, which may include economic growth, among different sub-regions within an economic union. An example of this is the ongoing adjustment of inequities within the EC regarding southern Italy, Scotland, and other economically depressed regions. Internal regional dependence within the EC is, in actuality, an attempt to even out the disparities in such areas as wage and employment levels between the more advanced European regions of north-eastern France and the Rhine Valley and the low-income regions such as Ireland. Regional inequalities of this type are generally analysed within the theory of regional integration and should not be confused with the theory of dependence.

The Governing Conditions of European Regional Dependence

The term regional dependence describes the reliance of a region and its sub-unit states on some external region. Regional dependence is not necessarily internally structured. Members of a region could conceivably find that their region has developed a certain type of trade or economic dependence on another region, or vice versa. Regional dependence can be intentional. For example, during the nineteenth century the European powers pursued a clear-cut colonial policy in other regions designed to result in a structure of dominance and dependence. To cite another example, the United States (if one considers it as a region) sought after the Second World War to foster European financial dependence on the US dollar.

Four conditions must exist in order for regional dependence to develop. A brief discussion of each is presented here.

External Reliance

The first governing condition is external reliance. In this context, it means some form of dependent relationship in trade, aid, and culture. Such a relationship must be regionally discernible, but the two regions need not develop trade relations alone in order to satisfy the definition of regional dependence. For example, the Arab world and Africa could be described as regionally dependent, although the bulk of Africa's trade is not directed toward the Arab world.[1] Such interdependence can be seen as political, cultural, and economic.

Two regions need not necessarily exchange goods and services in order to be dependent. South-East Asia (for example Malaysia and Indonesia) has been influenced by Arab–Islamic culture in the past and can be said to be regionally dependent on it.

The Existence of Rewards

For any relationship of regional dependence to be described as such, rewards must be derived from it by both partners, although not necessarily equally. That is aid, or the unrequited transfer condition, must be fulfilled. Relationships that are based solely on hegemony of one party over another are not dependent *per se*, but require the application or the threatened application of force or coercion in order for the relationship to be maintained. As a result, choice is ruled out; analysts should look upon these kinds of relationships, even if they are economically based, as forms of dominance rather than dependence.

The presence of mutual rewards in a regionally dependent relationship involves a cost for the two parties, but the cost must not exceed the benefits for either party if the relationship is to be rationally justified. Even in relationships where reward and cost are theoretically equal, the relationship may still be a strong one, since the area of choice of substitutable dependent relationships may be very limited.

Absence of Measurable Military Interaction

The third condition for the existence of regional dependence is the absence of any measurable military interaction. The presence of such interaction would negate the regional character of the relationship through the creation of military blocs and alliances based on the powers of nation states and not on regions. Most such alliances are characterized by the one-way flow of goods (say, in procurement) and the dominance of a single power, for example the US in NATO and the USSR in the Warsaw Pact. Hegemony and unidirectional flows limit the flexibility of interaction and tend to make reversals of direction costly in the short run.

Limited or marginal sales of military goods may, however, cause a dependence that began as regional to develop into a *de facto* alliance, especially during crisis situations. To eliminate this factor in this study, the time period of 1971–9 was intentionally constructed in order to avoid the inclusion of the Soviet invasion of Afghanistan or the Iraq–Iran war. These two crises may have already produced alliances that are not yet readily apparent or that lend themselves to rational explanations.

Relative Economic Equity

Just as military interaction constrains regional dependence relationships, so does the existence of a substantial economic gap between the two parties. In order for the dependence relationship to survive over a period of time and be manageable, the two parties should not be extreme opposites in terms of wealth, power, and prestige, or else opportunities for coercion would displace those for negotiation.

Two groups of countries could not be at opposite ends of the international power hierarchy and be studied within this paradigm. For example, one cannot say that a regional dependence exists between the two regions of North America and the Arab world. Discrepancies in wealth and in economic and military power eliminate any measurable bargaining power. A similar situation exists in any interaction between the Soviet Union and the Arab world.

The theory of regional dependence, therefore, must be discussed in terms of understanding and analysis of the interaction between 'medium' powers, or interactions between groups of smaller and relatively non-powerful states on a regional basis. It is assumed that in this type of relationship the use of force to regulate such dependence is eliminated and, hence, the semi-co-operative nature of the relationship is preserved.

Reciprocity

In addition to the four essential conditions discussed above, the relationship may exhibit some form of reciprocity. This allows decision makers on both sides to manipulate to some degree the exchange of the rewards that result from it. However, this is not necessarily a condition for the existence of regional dependence at the international level. Some degree of reciprocity, although it may not necessarily be symmetrical, enhances bartering power among regions and perhaps leads to a more stable relationship over the long term.

The Emerging Trade Dependence of Europe on the Arab World

In examining EC relations with the Arab world one can find some of the preceding conditions in effect, and can also discern a historically determined pattern of trade and aid flow. The EC receives an average of 52.4 per cent of its fuel needs from the Arab world (see Table 3.1). In addition, the EC directs 15.83 per cent (in 1980) of its exports to the Arab world. Such an export profile (as shown in Table 3.2) indicates that the Arab market, both traditionally and as a result of recent, unprecedented growth, has been a major outlet for EC goods

Table 3.1. Percentage Share of European Community Dependence
on Arab Fuel Products (1963-1981)

Year	Per cent	
1963	50	
1973	62	
1978	56	Mean = 52.4%
1979	52	
1981	42	

Sources: General Agreement on Tariffs and Trade (GATT), *International Trade, 1979-80* (Geneva, GATT, 1980), Table A-3. Commission of the European Communities, Directorate-General for Economic and Financial Affairs, *European Economy*, No. 8 (Brussels, March 1981), Table 22.

and services. In 1980, for instance, EC imports to the region reached an all-time high of $49.7 billion.

In terms of imports, the EC's overall imports from the Arab region have experienced a phenomenal increase in absolute dollar values and as a percentage of total EC imports. Notwithstanding inflationary effects and currency fluctuations, Europe as a region increased its total imports from the Arab world from $9.7 billion in 1971 to $83 billion in 1980. (See Table 3.2.) This meant an absolute increase in the percentage of the Arab share of the value of EC imports from 15.33 in 1971 to 21.83 in 1980. (See Table 3.5.)

Just as the EC is heavily dependent on the Arab world for fuel, so is the Arab world largely dependent on the EC for procurement of manufactured goods, engineering goods, and services. As can be demonstrated from the figures shown in Table 3.3, an average of 86.8 per cent of EC exports to the Arab world is in manufactured goods, of which an average of 58.5 per cent is engineering products. However, the lessening of EC dependence on Arab oil products is not equally reflected in a comparable lessening of Arab dependence on EC manufacturers. Available statistics for the latter reveal a mere three percentile decrease between 1973 and 1979.

In the financial sphere of Euro–Arab relations, the Arab world deposits a major portion of its official and private holdings in European banks. The Bank for International Settlements has calculated that the size of those deposits has increased in dollar value from $55.1 billion at the end of 1976 to $106.2

Table 3.2. European Community Exports and Imports to/from the Arab World 1961–1980*
(in current $US billions)

	1961	1969	1973	1974	1975	1976	1977	1978	1979	1980
Exports to the Arab world										
EC exports	2.54	3.45	8.45	12.79	19.26	21.71	27.35	32.45	40.97	49.65
Total extra-EC exports	30.43	55.64	125.75	136.27	150.43	158.06	187.41	222.66	265.76	313.58
EC exports as a percentage of total extra-EC exports	8.34	6.20	6.72	9.39	12.81	13.73	14.59	14.57	15.42	15.83
Imports from the Arab world										
EC imports	3.51	8.62	14.91	34.64	31.71	35.34	37.43	37.61	55.58	82.96
Total extra-EC imports	28.97	46.91	103.66	156.18	155.60	178.43	195.98	227.32	298.97	379.95
EC imports as a percentage of total extra-EC imports	12.13	18.37	14.38	22.18	19.74	19.81	19.10	16.55	18.59	21.83

*Excludes Jibuti and includes Danish and British exports and imports throughout the period.
Source: International Monetary Fund, *Direction of Trade Statistics Annual* (Washington DC, IMF, 1963, 1967, 1971, 1978, 1981).

Table 3.3. Percentage Shares of Manufactured Goods and Engineering
Products in Total European Community Exports to the
Arab World (1973-1979)

	1973	1977	1978	1979
Manufactured goods	87.1	86.9	87.8	84.4
Percentage of which were engineering products	55.3	61.8	60.6	56.3

Source: General Agreement on Tariffs and Trade (GATT), *International Trade, 1979-80* (Geneva, GATT, 1980), Table A-19.

billion at the end of 1979. Such a huge flow of Arab money
helps to rectify deficits in EC payments and sustain the growth
of the Euro–Arab trading bloc.[2]

Furthermore, the Arab world receives a high percentage of
EC bilateral and multilateral official aid commitments. Table
3.4 shows that EC aid commitments to the Arab world have
declined over the period 1961-77. The Arab world received
38.14 per cent of total EC aid in 1961. With the independence
of many Arab countries and the expansion of internal Arab
production of raw material, especially oil, the percentage of
that aid declined significantly in the 1960s. As shown in Table
3.4, the decline of EC aid has, however, moderated in the
1970s.

European Regional Dependence and Aid

Many theorists of dependence have examined the concept of
aid concentration as an index of the dependence of the LDCs
on their former 'mother' countries. In so doing, they measured
the association (or correlation) between aid concentration
over time and economic growth in some LDCs.[3] In this study,
the opposite approach is taken—that of measuring the motives
behind the allocation of West European foreign aid and determining the correlation of this with other factors of regional
dependence. The aim of such analysis is to determine whether
there are any factors behind the allocation of developmental
assistance by EC members to the resource-poor states of the
Arab world over a given period of time.

The extension of official development assistance by wealthy

Table 3.4. European Community Net Official Development Assistance to Arab Countries (1961–1977)*
(in $US millions)

Country	1961	1962	1963	1964	1965	1966	1967	1968	1969	1970	1971	1972	1973	1974	1975	1976	1977
Algeria	398.9	314.17	213.1	161.24	127.07	106.99	94.54	—	112.7	105.8	98.9	87.4	82.3	91.2	102	112.2	94.8
Bahrain	0.94	1.35	0.64	0.80	0.88	0.88	0.05	—	0.1	0.3	0.3	0.6	0.5	0.6	0.7	0.7	0.9
Egypt	0.31	0.87	1.06	2.82	2.83	3.38	4.03	—	3.9	40.9	10	6.6	26.9	56.4	110.2	114.9	94.5
Iraq	0.02	0.14	0.09	0.70	0.74	0.88	0.61	—	0.6	1.5	0.5	0.7	0.9	1.0	1.3	0.9	1.0
Jordan	8.22	6.27	6.32	7.0	7.07	5.78	7.2	—	8.2	5.7	10.2	21.8	15.2	21.6	34	31.1	28.1
Kuwait	—	—	—	—	—	—	—	—	0.1	—	—	—	—	—	—	—	—
Lebanon	0.11	0.15	0.14	0.30	0.69	0.73	0.79	—	1.0	2.6	2.4	2.9	2.9	4.6	6.7	9.2	6.5
Libya	12.52	11	9.59	11.14	4.18	2.29	2.11	—	4.7	2.8	1.8	5.2	10.8	10.2	0.4	6.2	5.1
Mauritania	0.02	—	-0.01	9.03	9.49	4.35	7.58	—	4.9	3.5	2.3	3.1	10.4	12.8	8.1	11.3	14.3
Morocco	12.54	13.9	19.12	18.46	19.97	21.59	17.72	—	44.0	38.3	58.9	48.9	53.5	51.1	152.8	116.2	111.9
Oman	0.36	0.44	0.38	4.06	0.10	0.64	0.94	—	0.1	0.1	—	—	0.3	0.5	0.6	0.7	0.5
Qatar	—	0.01	—	0.02	0.03	0.04	0.04	—	—	—	0.3	0.4	0.3	0.6	0.2	0.1	1.5
Saudi Arabia	19.39	13.8	16.31	10.98	17.19	9.26	5.96	—	19.4	15	14.6	8.5	18.2	7.0	11.3	10.5	18.2
Somalia	0.01	0.24	0.76	0.84	0.76	1.03	0.99	—	2.1	-0.2	-0.9	6.1	11.9	27.4	45.2	48.1	43.9
Sudan	0.24	0.32	0.164	0.54	0.88	1.25	0.78	—	0.7	3.1	1.1	0.7	1.3	4.7	3.3	18	4
Syria	15.13	15	16.80	16.7	17.54	18.36	15.32	—	44.5	47.2	44.6	52.1	80.8	80.1	80.9	120.8	133.1
Tunisia	0.54	0.43	0.39	0.33	1.49	1.30	1.57	—	1.7	4.7	9	9	12.3	20.2	9.8	11	25.6
UAE	—	0.16	0.24	0.8	0.78	0.44	0.07	—	1.5	1.2	2	1.6	1.7	3.8	4.4	2.7	5.6
South Yemen	8.9	11.17	13.18	16.63	25.98	30.20	22.92	—									
Total EC aid to Arab countries	478.19	398.95	298.77	261.4	237.65	209.39	183.22	—	250.9	272.3	255.2	254.5	329	392.2	570.4	613.6	587
Total EC aid	1,253.77	1,274.85	1,205.87	1,237.59	1,313.16	1,266.82	1,356.35	—	1,991.2	2,090.8	2,400.2	2,613.3	3,009.3	3,517.4	4,302.7	4,391.2	4,588.2
Per cent†	38.14	30.59	24.78	21.12	18.10	16.53	13.51	—	12.60	13.02	10.6	9.67	10.93	11.15	13.26	13.97	12.97

*Excludes Jibuti and includes British and Danish aid to Arab countries in the period 1961–73.
†Total EC aid to Arab countries as a percentage of total EC aid.
Source: OECD–DAC, *Geographic Distribution of Financial Flows to Developing Countries* (Paris, OECD–DAC, 1965, 1966, 1968, 1975, 1978).

countries to less-developed ones is unquestionably partly humanitarian. However. historical precedent and academic studies have both shown that European economic assistance to developing countries (especially British aid) in the post-war era reflects East–West competition as well as commercial interests.[4]

It is also tempting to argue that European financial assistance and contributions to nations which were or had been colonies may also reflect a sense of psychological and mercantilist interest, or dependence. However, this suggestion is conjecture and should be subjected to empirical tests on another occasion. For the purposes of this study, the emphasis is on EC aid policies towards the Arab world during the period 1961–77.

The hypothesis for this study is that aid is a reflection of economic dependence or, that EC member states tend to allocate foreign aid to underdeveloped regions according to a perception of the political and/or economic importance of those regions. Stated another way, EC member states attempt to influence the economic policies of oil-rich Arab states through economic aid to resource-poor Arab states. This relationship can be illustrated, as in the following diagram, as consisting of a triad involving the three parties.

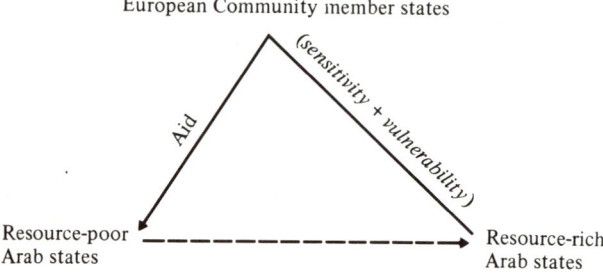

The problem, then, is to find some association over a given period of time (in this case between 1961 and 1977) between the variables of aid to the Arab region and the price of the products generated by that region. One can establish, through linear regression analysis, that EC member states provide development aid to inflence not only the recipient Arab states but also to influence the decisions of their wealthy Arab neighbour states. Through examination of the correlates, one comes closer to understanding the evolving substance of associative diplomacy.[5]

The given relationship takes the following linear regression form:

$$y = a + b_1 x_1 + b_2 x_2 + b_3 x_3 + b_k x_k$$

where y = value of EC member's aid concentration to the Arab world,[6] measured in the form of the percentage:

$$\frac{\text{EC members' official aid to Arab states}}{\text{all EC members' official aid}} \times 100,$$

a = a constant measuring EC members' aid commitments if all other variables in the equation are equal to zero,

$b_1, b_2 \therefore$ = rates of change of y with respect to variables x_1, x_2, x_3 or the slopes of variables x_1, x_2, x_3,

x_1 = EC import quotient (Value of EC imports from the Arab world as a percentage of total extra-EC imports),[7]

x_2 = oil price quotient (the oil price index as a percentage of all LDCs' export price index),[8]

x_3 = Arab raw material price quotient (the Arab raw material price index as a percentage of all LDCs' export price index, 1970 = 1.00).[9]

Table 3.5 and Figures 3.1 to 3.4 give the data as percentages; other data pertaining to total aid and total imports are given in the appendices.

Preliminary Examination of Table 3.5

Table 3.5 shows EC members' assistance allocations to twenty Arab nations, members of the Arab League. It shows all official assistance, both bilateral and multilateral, except EC aid programmes that were administered through the UN. It does not include military aid. The twenty Arab states include all of the countries of the Mahgreb and the Mashreq, along with Mauritania, Somalia, and other states that are members of the Arab League, except for Palestine and Jibuti.

An examination of the concentration of EC aid over the period encompassed by this study (1961–77) reveals that EC

Table 3.5. A Regression Table of European Community Aid to the Arab World (1961–1977)*

Year	EC aid concentration	EC import quotient per cent	Oil price quotient	Arab raw material price quotient
1961	38.14	12.13	1.11	1.13
1962	30.50	12.63	1.11	1.11
1963	24.78	12.55	1.09	1.11
1964	21.12	12.75	1.09	1.11
1965	18.10	12.57	1.03	1.07
1966	16.53	12.65	1.01	1.06
1967	13.51	13.06	1.02	1.03
1968	–	18.68	1.03	1.03
1969	12.60	18.37	1.00	1.03
1970	13.02	17.77	1.00	1.00
1971	10.60	15.33	1.17	0.89
1972	9.67	14.58	1.18	0.90
1973	10.93	14.38	1.19	0.90
1974	11.15	22.18	1.17	0.59
1975	13.26	19.74	1.88	0.55
1976	13.97	19.81	1.90	0.62
1977	12.79	19.10	1.83	0.72

*Includes United Kingdom and Danish aid to Arab countries and excludes Jibuti.
Source: OECD–DAC, *Eurostat: Monthly External Trade Bulletin 1958–1979* (Paris, OECD–DAC, 1980).

aid concentration declined measurably in the 1960s; that trend began to reverse in about 1972 and became more stable from 1973 to the end of the period (1977). EC imports from the Arab world increased progressively throughout the period, suggesting that the Arab world had become a major trade partner with the EC. (See Figures 3.1 and 3.2.)

The oil price quotient seems to have declined marginally in the 1960s, and then that decline reversed in around 1971 (Figure 3.3). Oil price quotient statistics seem to be somewhat conservative, possibly because they are measured in 1970 prices and are based on all raw materials exported from underdeveloped countries rather than on the oil price quotient as an isolated factor. We know, of course, that oil prices quadrupled

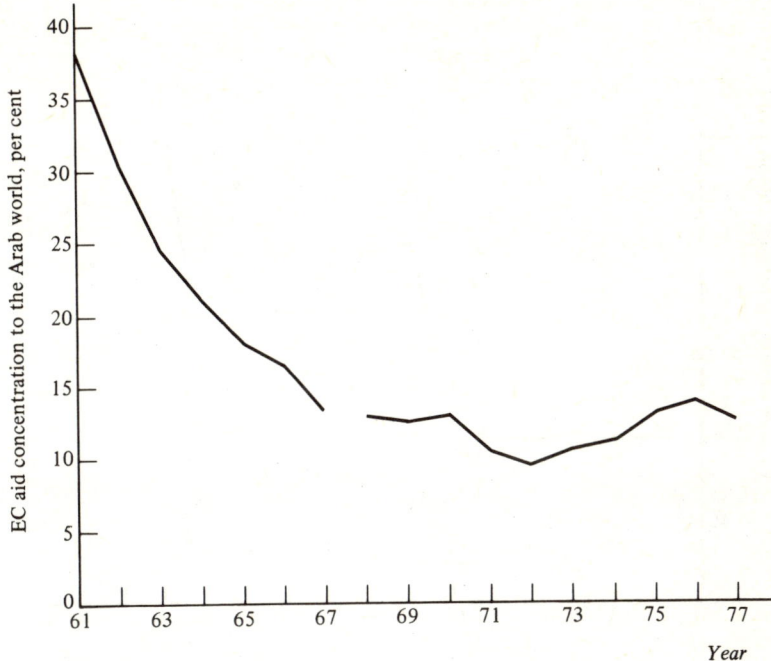

Fig. 3.1. European Community Aid Concentration to the Arab World (1961–1977).

in 1974, but our statistics do not fully reflect this. This observation leads one to question whether the prices of raw materials have outpaced the prices of other goods. However, the answer to this question is outside the scope of this study. The question is introduced here because of its relevance to the conservative nature of this measurement, which tends to minimize statistically the association between aid and oil prices during the period of time under study. The fourth variable—the Arab raw material price quotient—seems, however, largely to decline throughout the entire period (Figure 3.4).

When the oil price quotient and the Arab raw material quotient are compared, an inverse relationship is apparent throughout virtually the entire time period. It is significant to note that all of the measurements have been expressed in terms of quotients, or percentages and that the last two variables (oil prices and Arab raw material prices) have been

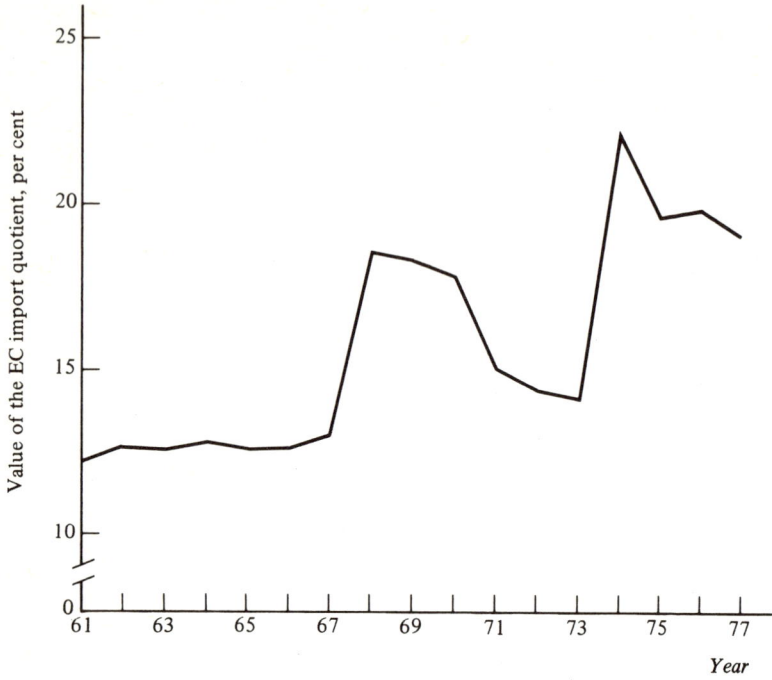

Fig. 3.2. The European Community Import Quotient (1961–1971).

measured in terms of 1970 prices. This has been done in an attempt to deflate the model and to purge inflationary pressures from the regression and from the resulting correlation.

Correlates of EC Members' Aid to the Arab World (1961–77)

In this subsection the hypothesis (that EC member states tend to concentrate their aid on the resource-poor Arab states in order to produce positive regional economic policies) will be tested. Hypothetically, EC members expect that aid to the resource-poor Arab states would produce positive and favourable reactions by Arab countries towards Europe, including effects on the oil-pricing policies of the wealthier Arab states.

   To prove such an assumption, it is necessary to correlate over time, or regress, EC aid concentration with four independent variables: (1) the value of the EC import quotient; (2) the oil price quotient, given 1970 = 1 (or base year); (3) the

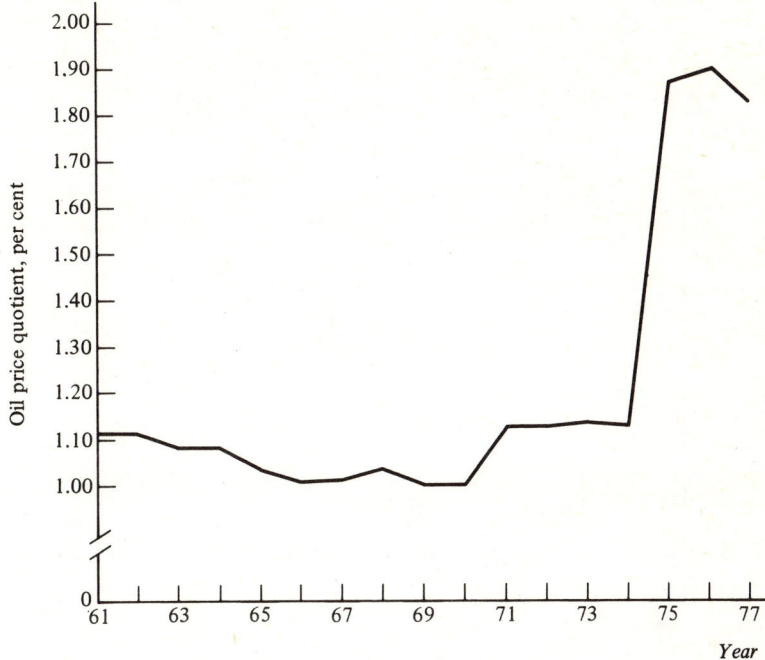

Fig. 3.3. The Oil Price Quotient (1961–1977).

Arab raw material price quotient exported, also expressed in relation to the prices of LDC exports, and given 1970 = 1; and (4) these factors in relationship to the years under study—1961–77.

EC aid concentration is considered the dependent variable, and the EC import quotient, the oil price quotient, the Arab raw material price quotient, and the years under study are each considered independent variables.

Thus:

EC aid concentration = f (EC import quotient, oil price
raw material price quotient, year)
+ U,

where

U is a function of other variables.

As is indicated in Table 3.6, the analysis anticipated that EC

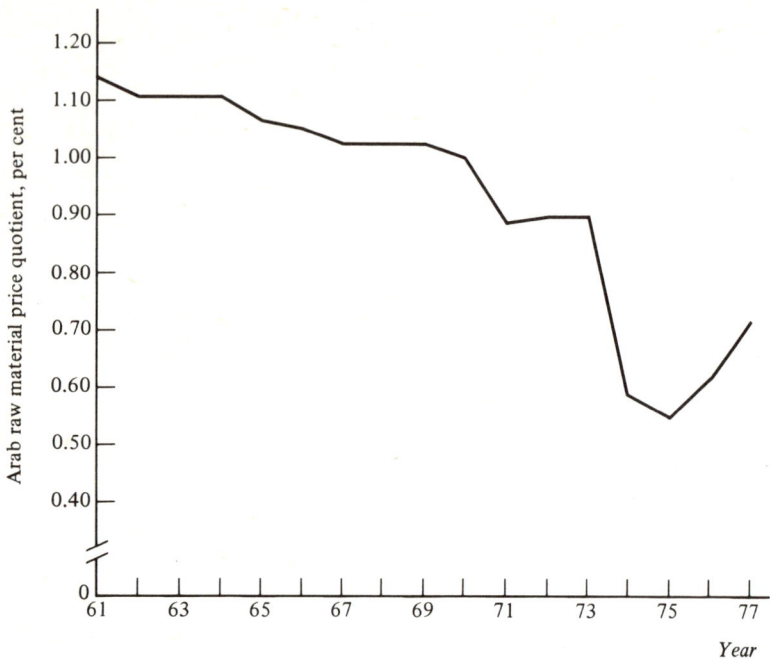

Fig. 3.4. The Arab Raw Material Price Quotient (1961-1977).

members' aid commitment to the Arab world would tend to increase as a result of increases in the members' dependence on imports from the Arab world. However, the regression indicates that although a moderate relationship exists between the EC import quotient and EC aid concentration ($R^2 = 0.3514$), the influence of EC imports on EC aid concentration tended to be negative and of a magnitude of 7 per cent ($b = -0.6958$). The level of significance of the inclusion of this variable in the equation (f) is small ($f = 0.159$), suggesting that the measurement of this variable in aid is not highly reliable, i.e. is not at the 0.05 level of reliability. (See Table 3.7.)

In correlating the second and main variable in our aid concentration equation (oil price quotient) to aid, the predicted association is positive, and the result is positive, indicating a strong association of 40 per cent between changes in the price of oil and the allocation of aid by EC members to the Arab region ($R^2 = +0.4023$). In fact, the computer regression indicates that EC aid to the Arab states tended to increase by

Table 3.6. Correlations and Measures of Variability Among Indicators of European Community Members' Aid Concentration to the Arab World (1961–1977)

Indicator	EC aid concentration	Value of EC import quotient	Oil price quotient	Arab raw material price quotient	*Year*
Aid concentration	1.00	–	–	–	–
Value of EC import quotient	–0.59	1.00	–	–	–
Oil price quotient	–0.13	0.54	1.00	–	–
Arab raw material price quotient	0.44	–0.80	–0.80	1.00	–
Year	–0.67	0.79	0.70	0.89	1.00
Mean range	15.93%	15.78%	1.22%	0.93%	
Low	9.67%	12.13%	1.00%	0.55%	
High	38.14%	22.18%	1.90%	1.13%	
Standard deviation	8.78%	3.33%	0.31%	0.19%	
Coefficient of variability	55.1%	21.1%	25.7%	20.9%	
Number of cases	16	17	17	17	

Table 3.7. Correlation and Measures of Linear Regression of European Community Members' Aid Concentration to the Arab World (1961–77)

Indicators	Value of EC import quotient	Oil price quotient	Arab raw material price quotient
Predicted association	+	+	+
R^2	0.3514	0.4023	0.4241
Adjusted R^2	0.3082	0.3169	0.3545
b	–0.6958	13.7119	–23.8081
a	–0.2635	0.4919	–0.5273
f	0.159	3.516	1.406
Adjusted f^*	0.803	9.892†	0.274
Degrees of freedom	4 and 12	4 and 12	4 and 12
Number of cases	17	17	17

*Pertaining to normal distribution of data through z-score transformation.

†Significant correlation at the 0.1 per cent level of significance for one-tail critical distribution of f (4 and 12 degrees of freedom).

14 per cent whenever the price of oil increased by 100 per cent (b = 13.7119). The level of significance of this measure is moderate (f = 3.516), suggesting that with 4 and 12 degrees of freedom there is a significant measure of association at 0.05 probability.

The correlation of the third variable (the Arab raw material price quotient) with EC aid results in a strong association of 42 per cent (R^2 = 0.4241). However, unexpectedly, the increase in the price of Arab raw materials tended to affect EC aid allocation negatively by some 24 per cent (b = 23.8081). Such a result suggests that either the Arab world is not considered by EC members as an important source of raw materials, or that increases in the prices of raw materials may enhance the ability of an underdeveloped country to meet its financial obligations, hence the EC countries, as aid donors, concentrate their aid to states that cannot adequately finance their imports. The level of significance (at 0.05 probability) is not, however, high (f = 1.406).

Correlation of EC aid concentration over the given period (1961–77) shows that aid concentration varied greatly over the time period (R^2 = 0.6949). Contrary to expectations, EC aid concentration tended to decrease by 2 per cent per year (b = 2.2328). However, such a decrease seems to have moderated after 1970 (f = 13.73).

In sum, EC aid concentration over the given period of time tended to correlate positively with oil prices and inversely with the EC imports from the Arab world and with the prices of Arab raw materials. EC aid concentration also tended to decrease marginally over time; however, it tended to decrease more progressively in the 1960s than in the 1980s.

Oil Price Quotient: The Salient Factor in EC Aid Concentration (1961–1977)

In attempting to isolate the variable that was most important in determining EC aid concentration to the Arab world, a regression equation was constructed, given these constraints: (1) 5 variables; (2) 17 cases; (3) a significant level represented by f value of 2.0 and tolerance value of 0.10—that is, rejected any variation in association of less than 10 per cent.

The result has shown repeatedly that aid concentration tended to be associated over time with the oil price quotient

(R^2 = 0.3514). Table 3.7 shows that the f statistic ($f_{oil - aid}$ = 15.94) is significant at a level of significance of approximately 0.01 with 2 and 14 degrees of freedom.

From the previously described regression analysis, research has shown that there was a strong association between oil price increases and increases in aid allocations from EC members to resource-poor Arab states in the period 1961–77, and that such an association became more pronounced after 1971.

Comments

While the regression analyses of the policies of EC members toward the Arab world were based on a statistically small number of observations (over a period of 17 years), this period of time was particularly significant from a historical standpoint. During these years, cold-war antagonism in Europe decreased, Arab oil emerged as a strategic commodity, and associative diplomacy on the part of EC members toward the Arab world had its start.

In Chapters 4 and 5 the content of interviews with the EC secretariat in Brussels will confirm this statistical association of aid and oil prices as hypothesized here, and will show that the EC member states tend to follow a regional political/ economic policy toward the Arab world.

Aid and Associative Diplomacy

The changes in the patterns of aid allocation which began to emerge in 1969 and continued throughout the 1970s indicate an awareness on the part of the EC member states of their vulnerability in terms of imports from the Arab world, particularly oil imports. Changes in the amounts of aid could, therefore, perhaps also be termed changes in the degree of dependence. However, the changes of direction of the association between aid and imports that occurred in around 1971 appear to signal a change in diplomatic relations, namely an effort to strengthen the numerous linkages and institutions that bind the EC to the Arab world. Such a change in diplomatic relations is largely, but not solely, the result of increased dependence.

The suggested regional dependence triad in which EC members channelled their aid allocations to resource-poor Arab

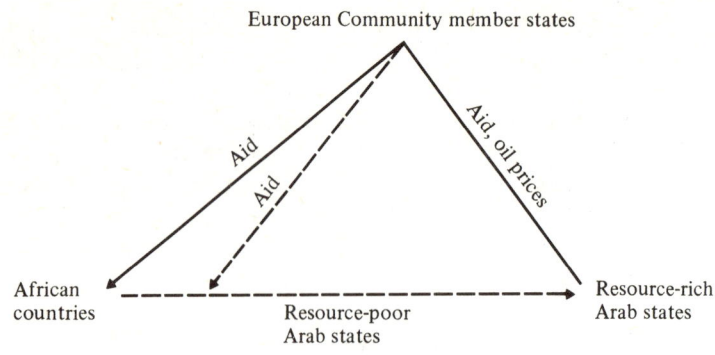

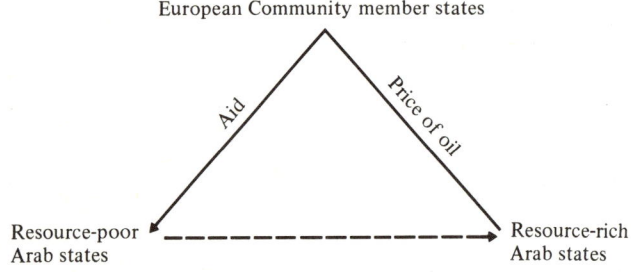

states in order to affect the prices of exports from resource-rich Arab states seems to be holding. However, the direction of aid commitments seems to have changed. The rich Arab states have also begun to direct their aid commitment through EC channels. The triad may also have increased in size to cover the African states as well. The two diagrams illustrate the new shift. The second diagram illustrates a new form of associative diplomacy based on aid (this time Arab and EC) that developed in the late 1970s and early 1980s. This development will be addressed in Chapter 6.

Notes

1. See V. LeVine and T. W. Luke, *The Arab–African Connection: Political and Economic Realities* (Boulder, Colo., Westview Press, 1979).
2. Those banks also include Swedish, Swiss, and Austrian banks as well as EC banks. See Bank for International Settlements, *Fiftieth Annual Report, April 1, 1979–March 31, 1980* (Basle, Switzerland, 9 June 1980), p. 155.
3. See V. A. Mahler, *Dependency Approaches to International Political*

Economy, A Cross-National Study (New York, Columbia University Press, 1980), Chapter 3.

4. In a study of German, French, and British aid policies for 1964 and 1967, Eugene Wittkopf has found a positive correlation between their aid commitments toward the Arab world during these years and the size of their trade with the Arab countries receiving aid. See Wittkopf, *Western Bilateral Aid Allocation: A Comparative Study of Recipient State Attributes and Aid Received* (Beverly Hills, Sage Professional Paper No. 02–005, Vol. 1, 1972), p. 24.

5. Statistically, multiple regression analysis and correlation can be examined in T. Anderson and M. Zelditch (jun), *A Basic Course in Statistics with Sociological Applications* (New York, Holt, Rinehart, and Winston, 1975). For utilizing computer models for the solution of multiple regression, I have adopted Norman Nie's method in Nie *et al., Statistical Package for the Social Sciences (SPSS)* (2nd edn, New York, McGraw-Hill, 1975).

6. EC aid commitments are from Organization for Economic Co-operation and Development, *Geographic Distribution of Financial Flows to Developing Countries* (Paris, OECD–DAC, issues 1965–78).

7. Data for the value of the EC imports from the Arab world were derived from International Monetary Fund, *Direction of Trade Statistics Annual (1980)*, and from *Eurostat: Monthly External Trade Bulletin, 1958-1979* (Brussels, OECD–DAC, 1980).

8. These data were provided by the United Nations, *World Trade Statistical Indexes* (New York, UN, issues 1961-77), providing 1970 = 1 as a deflationary measure. See also UN, *Statistical Yearbook* (New York, UN, 1974), Table 15.

9. UN, op. cit.

PART II

THE STRUCTURE AND PROCESSES OF ASSOCIATIVE DIPLOMACY

4 THE EURO–ARAB DIALOGUE

In the aftermath of the 1973 Arab–Israeli war both the Arabs and the Western Europeans realized the need for a new structure of diplomacy—one that was regionally based and broadly enough oriented to encompass many areas of mutual concern. As a result, the Euro–Arab Dialogue was initiated in March 1974 and has since evolved into a more institutionalized approach, in which representatives from both groups, through general and specialized committees of experts, have worked to attain both regional and inter-regional objectives.

A number of interrelated events took place during and soon after October 1973. The more neutral position of Western Europe[1] in the Arab–Israeli conflict of October 1973, the threatened oil embargo of Europe, and the consequent rise in oil prices, made it necessary and even logical for the two sides to contemplate regional co-operation. As a consequence, at a meeting of the nine European Community (EC) member countries in Brussels on 6 November 1973, the foreign ministers of the member countries issued a joint declaration on the Middle East in which they reaffirmed:

> . . . the ties of all kinds which have long linked the Europeans to the countries of the southern and eastern Mediterranean. In this connection, they reaffirm the terms of the declaration of the Paris Summit of 21 October 1972 and recall that the Community is determined to negotiate agreements with those countries within the framework of a balanced, overall approach.[2]

The intent of the Europeans to proceed with some form of dialogue with the Arab states, coupled with their declared neutrality in the October 1973 war, brought about a positive response from heads of Arab states. Meeting in Algeria on 28 November 1973, representatives at the Arab summit meeting adopted a special declaration directed to the EC countries which again restated the historic bonds that link the two groups of countries and asked the Europeans to lift their embargo on arms sales to the Arab world. The Arab leaders declared their readiness to begin discussions with the Europeans as soon as possible.[3]

Origins of the Euro-Arab Dialogue

The Euro-Arab Dialogue (EAD) was conceived initially by the French and the idea was explored in contacts with Libya prior to the outbreak of the 1973 war. The French leadership, in an attempt to enhance France's prestige and establish a new network of relations between the North and the South, showed great faith in the effectiveness of personal contacts, which are well served by diplomatic interactions and dialogue.[4]

At a meeting on 26-7 November 1973 between French President Georges Pompidou and West German Chancellor Willy Brandt the two leaders reaffirmed European intentions to engage in a dialogue with the Arabs. In Cairo, Abdul-Salam Jalloud, the Libyan premier, actively enlisted support for a dialogue with the Europeans.[5]

Pompidou called for a European summit to discuss the Middle East crisis. This meeting took place in Copenhagen on 15 December 1973, and at that time four Arab foreign ministers (from Algeria, Tunisia, the Sudan, and the United Arab Emirates) came to Copenhagen to lay the foundation for a process of multilateral negotiations between the League of Arab States and members of the EC.

In the following two months France lobbied for, and succeeded in convincing its EC partners of the need to adopt, an independent approach toward the Arab world. The 4 March 1974 communiqué adopted by the EC Council of Ministers proposed the opening up of contacts and dialogue with the Arab states; the discussions were to encompass Euro-Arab co-operation in economic, technical, and cultural areas.

The six-point proposal, authored by Walter Scheel, West German foreign minister and president of the EC Council of Ministers, called for 'the political cooperation of the Nine and the European Economic Council' in efforts to put into effect periodic meetings of experts. The proposal suggested a possible meeting of the two groups at the foreign-minister level if such a meeting appeared to be worthwhile.[6]

The foreign ministers of the League of Arab States, meeting

in Tunis on 25–8 March, agreed to establish a nine-member delegation to negotiate with the EC on the forms and procedures of the proposed EAD. Initial contacts began in early April in Brussels, and the ensuing negotiations culminated in a major meeting in Paris in July 1974.

The Copenhagen summit asserted European independence *vis-à-vis* the US and committed the EC countries 'to assist in the search for peace and the guaranteeing of a settlement'.[7] In the meeting in Paris between Sheikh Subah Salim al Subah, the Kuwaiti Foreign Minister, Jean Sauvequarque, the French Foreign Minister, Mahmoud Riad, secretary-general of the League of Arab States, and M. Ortoli, president of the EC Commission, the parties agreed to begin the EAD discussion at the 'expert' level some time in 1975.[8]

A community of interest began to develop between Arab officials and experts and their European counterparts through a series of quasi-official meetings that took place in 1974–5. These meetings included the following conferences:

(1) The Le Monde Conference on Euro–Arab Co-operation, held in November 1973 and attended by a group of Arab and European officials in a non-official capacity. Present at this meeting was Libyan President Muammar al-Qaddafi;
(2) The Gaullist-Nasserite Conference in Tripoli, Libya, in March 1974;[9]
(3) The Milan Conference on Co-operation and Development in the Mediterranean Area, organized jointly by the Instituto Affair Internazionale in Rome and the EC.

Among those present at the Milan conference were Claude Cheysson, from the EC Commission for Development, Yusif Sayigh, a senior consultant to the Organization of Arab Petroleum Exporting Countries (OAPEC), Abedlouaa hab Keramane, a senior advisor to the Algerian Ministry of Industry and Energy, and Chedly Ayari, Tunisian Minister of National Economy.[10]

At the Milan conference, Cheysson declared the objectives of EC associative diplomacy and called for closer collaboration in the Mediterranean region, stating that:

. . . cooperation between the two banks of the Mediterranean will be to the economic, but not only economic, interests of both. Europe is the largest commercial market in the world. But since it is dependent on imported raw materials and since it does not aspire to the role of great military power (not having a very important political weight because of its excessive fragmentation), it would seem the ideal partner for a zone rich in raw materials, sources of energy, and manpower.[11]

The EC was thus presented to the conferees as an economic giant without military power—a mercantilist or 'civilian' power that should not be feared, and hence whose role was both propitious and desirable. Such were the emerging outlines of a collective EC policy of associative diplomacy toward the Arab world.

The unofficial Arab conferees, however, were for their part divided at the Milan conference over the best way to build a future relationship with the Europeans. Sayigh and Ayari enthused over a collaborative regional approach, while Boutros Ghali (at that time a professor at the University of Cairo) favoured bilateral economic (but not political) co-operation between Europe and the Arab world.[12]

Another important conference organized by the Interparliamentary Association for Euro–Arab Co-operation was held in Damascus on 14–17 September 1974, and was attended by approximately fifty-five European parliamentarians representing all of the parliaments of the EC countries except Denmark. The largest contingent at this conference came from Belgium, which was represented by fourteen delegates; twelve attended from Italy.[13] The political persuasions of the participants varied from country to country. The French delegation was dominated by the Gaullists, and the Italian delegation had representatives spanning the Italian political spectrum, including two representatives of the Italian Communist party. The meeting included representatives from nineteen Arab and European countries, and the agenda was far-ranging—including such issues as Euro–Arab industrial co-operation, and the recognition of Palestinian national rights, including the right to a homeland.

One result of the meeting was the establishment of a permanent Secretariat for Euro–Arab Co-operation, based in Paris. This organization has 350 members, and has met annually since 1974. It has been active in promoting a political climate favourable to the success of the official EAD, and regularly presents specific suggestions along these lines to the EC Council of Ministers. Members of the organization have also visited the US and have met with various Congressmen to explain the ramifications of the Palestinian question and the need for a change in US foreign policy regarding the Palestine Liberation Organization (PLO).[14]

Objectives of the EAD

Preliminary preparation for the dialogue between the EC and the League of Arab States took approximately eighteen months, during which the content of the dialogue and the level of representation on each side were determined. One of the most difficult problems to resolve was the representation of the Palestinians. However, at a meeting of the EC foreign ministers in Dublin on 11 February 1975, a formula was devised whereby each side was represented by a single delegation. This satisfied diplomatic imperatives on both sides, and established the regional character of the EAD.[15]

Each side had a certain set of objectives regarding the EAD. The Arabs insisted on the primacy of its political character, while the Europeans emphasized its economic nature. Overall, the Arabs sought to convince the EC to adopt even-handed policies in the region, and sought to gain European support for a negotiated Arab–Israeli settlement. As a means toward that end, the Arab delegates attempted to secure European diplomatic recognition of the PLO.

The concept of the EAD also appealed widely to all of the Arab states, rich and poor alike. For the resource-poor Arab states, the EAD was another means by which European economic aid could be acquired. Qualitative European aid—the transfer of technology, co-operation in nuclear development, and industrial training—was eagerly sought. In diplomatic terms, Arab states of all political persuasions saw in Europe a 'third alternative' through which they could gain some measure of support that might not be forthcoming from traditional big-power alliances.[16]

The wealthy Arab states sought to make their huge financial surpluses in Europe secure against such contingencies as the freezing of funds and delays in the remittal of profits, and hoped to inhibit the erosion of the value of their investments through some mechanism that would protect against inflation.

For the resource-poor Arab states, the availability of any form of foreign investment—be it Arab, European, or both—was of the highest priority.

For the Europeans, the EAD represented a chance to guarantee the continuous flow of petroleum from the Arab world, even at higher prices. Barring the attainment of this goal, the EC Commission would have settled for even an exchange of information regarding future production and shipments of oil. For the EC, the importance of the oil question gave the EAD its life-force. Apart from the question of oil supplies, the EAD was viewed by the Europeans as an important means of re-establishing a sphere of influence in the Arab region.[17] The EC also sought to direct Arab economic development away from heavy industry or capital-intensive industry, and toward intermediate industries in which the basic division of labour between Europe and the Arab world would be maintained.

A joint memorandum issued by the participants in the first joint export meeting of the EAD, held in Cairo on 14 June 1975, called for 'the development of basic and intermediate industries in the Arab countries', as well as 'effective flow of advanced European technology . . . on appropriate terms'.[18] The Europeans sought also to obtain advantages for their conglomerate corporations in the fast-growing construction markets of the Arab oil-producing states.[19] The Europeans, therefore, were utilizing an essentially supra-regional organization (the EAD) to further some regional interests. Finally, the Europeans sought to obtain formal Arab commitments to the financing of an international food programme for what Claude Cheysson called 'global food security'.[20]

The level of support for the EAD was not, however, unanimous on the part of either the Europeans or the Arabs. For example, Italy, France, and Ireland promoted the EAD, while Britain and West Germany oscillated in their support. Luxembourg and Belgium played increasingly active roles in the EAD. On the Arab side, Algeria, Tunisia, and the PLO supported the EAD from its outset, while Egypt, Saudi Arabia, and some of the Gulf states have tended to favour bilateral relations with the European states.[21]

The Structure of the EAD

The EAD is composed of twenty-one Arab states and ten West European countries, namely the ten EC countries. Each side is represented by a single delegation composed of ambassadors (since 1976) and experts in various fields.[22] These experts usually attend EAD meetings under the flags of the League of Arab States and the EC. The 'Dublin formula' provides for such representation in order to circumvent the controversial question of Palestinian representation, since the PLO is not recognized by the EC.

The EAD is divided into the General Committee at the ambassadorial level; seven working committees, each of which is made up of ten to fourteen experts from each side; and the political committee, composed of three senior-level representatives and two or three junior aides. The EC Commission and the secretariat of the League of Arab States are represented at the political level. Figure 4.1 shows the organization of the EAD committees and their areas of activity.

In November 1980 the two sides agreed to raise the level of representation to that of foreign ministers, and the first Euro–Arab general meeting of foreign ministers was scheduled to take place in October 1981.[23]

Initially, the EAD meetings in 1975 and 1976 were at the expert level. Names of members on the Arab side were proposed by their respective governments, and the EC experts were drawn from the staff of the EC Commission and from member states. However, frequent membership changes have prompted the secretary-general of the League of Arab States to suggest that experts be drawn from the ranks of specialized Arab League agencies rather than be nominated by the various national governments.[24]

The seven working committees of the EAD have usually met four or five times a year, while the General Committee has met once or twice a year. The most active year for the EAD was 1976, in which two major meetings of the General Committee and several small gatherings of experts were held. The most active committees have been the science and technology committee and the financial co-operation committee. (See Table 4.1.)

The science and technology committee has drawn up ten major projects, including detailed studies of a proposed curriculum

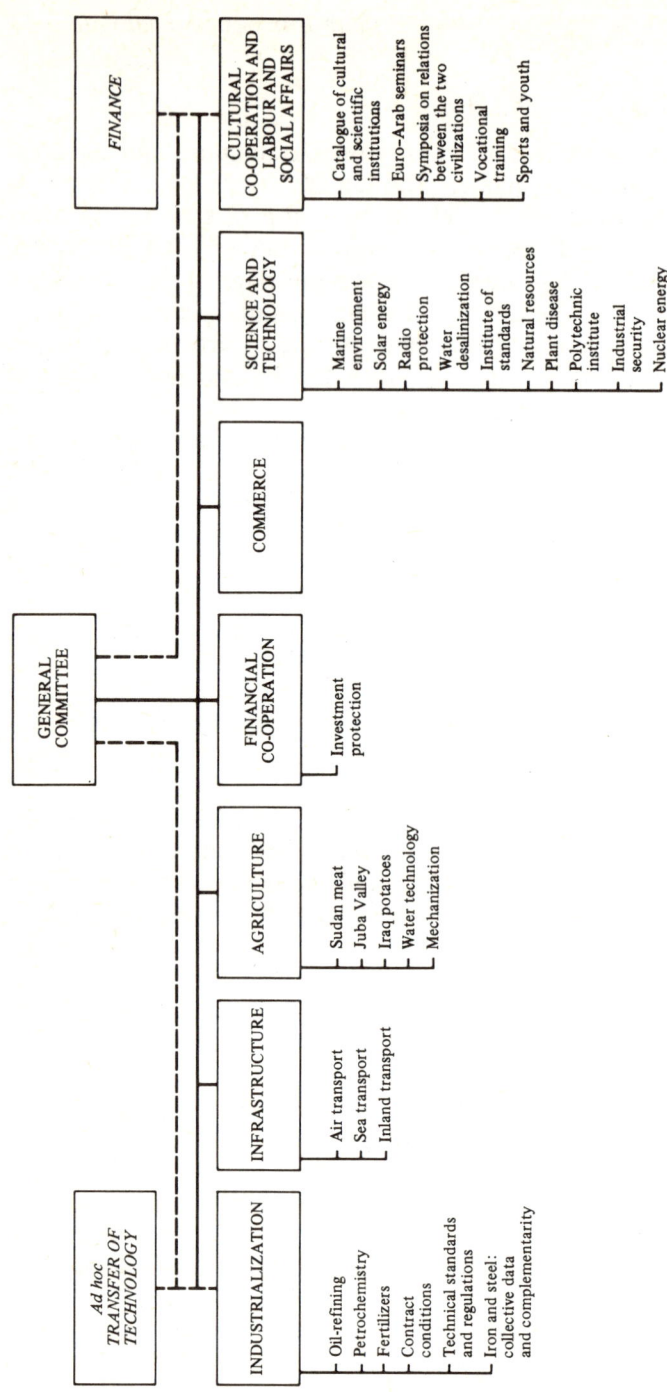

Fig. 4.1. Organization Chart of the Euro-Arab Dialogue Showing the Seven Working Committees and their Areas of Concentration.

Table 4.1. Meetings of the Euro-Arab Dialogue (1975–1980)

Location and date	Committee meetings								Other issues considered
	General	Industrial	Infrastructure	Agriculture	Finance	Trade	Science & technology	Cultural Labour	
Cairo, 4 June 1975*									
Rome, 24 July 1975		×	×	×	×		×	×	
Abu Dhabi, 27 November 1975		×	×	×	×	×	×		
Luxembourg, 20 May 1976			×	×	×		×	×	
Brussels, 2 June 1976	×								
Tunis, 12 February 1977	×			×	×	×	×	×	a*
Brussels, 28 October 1977	×	×	×	×	×	×	×	×	b*
Brussels, 8 December 1977							×		c*
Damascus, 11 December 1978	×	×	×	×	×	×	×	×	d
Luxembourg, 13 November 1980†									

*Preliminary meeting of experts.
†*Re* preparatory meeting.
a – Financing of the EAD.
b – Projects; lists and costs.
c – Single meeting.
d – Additional lists of projects.

for a Euro–Arab centre for technology in Kuwait. The financial co-operation committee has drafted a financial convention which calls for the prohibition of injurious action by any member state against the official and private assets of another member state. When EAD activities were temporarily suspended in late 1978, negotiations on the convention were in the final stages.[25]

The specific interests of the various Arab and European states in the activities of the EAD are reflected in the membership of the different committees and in the level of activity of individual countries on those committees. For example, Germany has consistently been represented on the industrialization committee and France on the infrastructure committee. Saudi Arabia, Kuwait, Abu Dhabi, and Britain have dominated the membership of the financial co-operation committee, while Belgium has been active on the science and technology committee. Italy and the PLO have consistently been represented on the cultural and labour committee. The commerce committee has met infrequently, and has been presided over on the European side by the Development Directorate of the EC Commission to ensure close monitoring of any commercial agreement that might impinge on the Commission's authority.[26]

The Evolution of the EAD

Since its inception in July 1975 the EAD has convened at least eight times; three of these meetings were at the expert level and five of them were at the ambassadorial level. In those meetings a number of issues were discussed and decided upon. Meeting places alternated between Arab and European capitals.

In general, the meetings of the experts were more productive than were the political meetings—or meetings attended by the different ambassadors. In the former, the experts from both sides were well prepared, and the meetings resulted in a number of studies and detailed projects. At the political level, ambassadors tended merely to reiterate earlier statements made by their respective foreign ministers or the declarations of summit meetings. The meetings were therefore ceremonial in nature, and no serious negotiations were conducted. This may have been due to the absence of sufficient authority on the part of the political representatives, and to the nature of the dialogue itself. The EAD often served as a sounding board or information-gathering channel for decisions adopted by higher governmental authorities at the quarterly meeting of the European Council or the League of Arab States' General Council.

First Expert Meeting in Cairo, 14 June 1975

This meeting dealt primary with the delineation of the general parameters and objectives of the EAD. Although the political nature of the dialogue was emphasized, in the eventual establishment of seven working committees there was no provision for a 'general political committee'. The joint memorandum released by the group at the conclusion of the meeting declared that: 'The Euro–Arab Dialogue is the product of a joint political will that emerged at the highest level with a view to establishing a special relationship between the two groups.'[27]

EAD advocates envisaged a future functional economic co-operation between the two regions that would contribute to stability, security, and a just resolution of the Palestinian problem. While the Europeans were prepared to co-operate economically with the Arabs, in 1975 they were not prepared to engage in multilateral political negotiations. This attitude was reflected in the stated caution of some European members, namely Britain and Germany, as well as in the insistence of US Secretary of State, Henry Kissinger, that the dialogue take place solely at the economic level.[28]

The seven working committees thus established were concerned with industrialization, basic infrastructure, agricultural and rural co-operation, trade, scientific and technological co-operation, and cultural and labour affairs. At the Cairo meeting it was also decided that a steering committee would be formed; this evolved a year later into the General Committee.

The Cairo meeting established the primacy of bilateral agreements concluded, or in negotiation, between the EC and individual Arab countries, as well as of those linking individual Arab countries with individual Western European countries. Bureaucratic and parochial fears were thus laid to rest. The Europeans gained from the Arabs an agreement to finance the UN World Food Programme while, in return, the Arabs received a promise of co-operation in the research and development of peaceful uses of nuclear energy.[29]

Second Expert Meeting in Rome, 24 July 1975

The Arabs persuaded the Europeans to conduct further EAD conferences at the ambassadorial level, without specifying a time for such an elevation of the talks. In Rome, each committee submitted a list of possible projects. The infrastructure committee agreed on a criterion for priority studies of projects that were of a regional development nature or that exceeded the capability of an individual Arab or European country.

In the finance committee the two sides engaged in serious negotiations concerning a code of investment guarantees. The Arabs contended that Arab funds invested in Europe—whether public or private—'belonged to nations rather than to individuals or companies'. The Europeans disagreed, arguing that all such funds were a 'patrimony of all countries concerned'.[30] In view of rumours concerning a secret US–Europe protocol that would limit the ability of Arab governments to manage their financial deposits in the US and in Europe, and in the light of US Senate hearings on the registration and monitoring of foreign investments, the Arab delegation was concerned about the protection of Arab investments from possible expropriation or freezing. The Arabs thus worked vigorously for an EC-wide measure assuring the protection of these investments from non-commercial risks.[31]

The Arab delegates further stressed the need for a stable currency exchange rate and sought European views on possible Arab investments denominated in European Units of Account (EUA). The two sides also agreed to co-operate more intensely in the monetary field, including the training of Arab experts at European financial institutions.[32]

Third Expert Meeting in Abu Dhabi, 27 November 1975

At the Abu Dhabi meeting the political dimensions of the EAD were reaffirmed, and both sides committed themselves to working out an agenda for future meetings at the ambassadorial level. The meeting took place against the backdrop of a low-profile visit to the Persian Gulf by US Assistant Secretary of the Treasury Gerald Parsky, who urged the Gulf states to refrain from discussing the issue of petroleum supplies with the Europeans.[33]

The final document summarizing the Abu Dhabi meeting

reinforced this point, stating: '. . . it being understood that crude oil and trading therein does not fall within the context of the dialogue because this matter is dealt with in other specialized international fora'.[34] The Arab side claimed that it was not going to delve into questions that might pre-empt the then ongoing North–South negotiations.

Some progress was made in the infrastructure committee on such specific projects as the enlargement of the Syrian seaport of Tartus, problems in construction of new towns and grain silos, and other issues. The agricultural committee discussed a programme for the expansion of wheat production in Syria and the production of potato seeds in Iraq. Feasibility studies were authorized for four projects.

In the matter of trade co-operation, the Arabs called for a multilateral trade agreement; the Europeans expressed some reservations on this, and argued that the EC Generalized System of Preferences already covered approximately 90 per cent of Arab exports to the EC countries. The Arabs, in turn, argued that while they appreciated European efforts toward trade promotion, they nevertheless recognized that the preference system was non-contractual and unilateral.

In the finance committee the Europeans agreed to compile a catalogue of financial training facilities in the various EC countries. The Arab side agreed that the principle of protection of investments against non-commercial risks was of the utmost importance. The Europeans presented the Arabs with a document describing different Western European laws and regulations affecting investments by foreigners. The Arabs sought some form of collective treaty to avoid double taxation; the Europeans responded that taxation treaties were best left for bilateral agreements between the respective national governments. The Europeans, however, stated that they welcomed limited Arab investments denominated in the EUA.[35]

In the finance committee the Arab members proposed joint financing of development projects in Europe and in the Arab world. The Europeans responded that due to budgetary constraints they were only capable of furnishing export credit guarantees and investment guarantees, and that such major financing must be left to the private sector.

In the science and technology committee the two sides exchanged information regarding the establishment of an Arab institute of technology in Syria and a polytechnic centre in Kuwait. The members discussed a possible curriculum for the electrical engineering department in the proposed Kuwait centre. The committee also discussed the preparation of geological maps utilizing remote-sensing and aerial photography. The Europeans expressed their readiness to help the Arabs set up an Arab information and documentation centre, and agreed to receive three to four Arab nuclear scientists for training in EC research centres.[36]

In the cultural and labour committee the two sides agreed to sponsor a seminar on the history of Euro–Arab relations, to be held in Italy, and another seminar on architecture and the problems of urban development, to be held in France.

First General Committee Meeting in Luxembourg,
18–20 May 1976

The first General Committee meeting of the Euro–Arab Dialogue took place at the ambassadorial level less than a year after the EAD was established and functioning at the expert level. The European delegation was chaired by Ambassador Jean Wagner of Luxembourg, representing the presidency of the European Political Co-operation System (EPCS) and the EC Council of Ministers, and by Dr Klaus Meyer, deputy secretary-general of the EC Commission, representing this body. The Arab delegation was chaired by Ambassador Abd el-Aziz al-Shamlan of Bahrain, representing the presidency of the Political Council of the League of Arab States, by Mahmoud Riyad, the secretary-general of the League of Arab States, and by Dr Ahmad Sedki al-Dajani, representing the PLO, which was a full member of the League of Arab States.

The Luxembourg meeting was important since it elevated the level of representation and brought the political aspects of the EAD to the fore. In the meeting the Arabs succeeded in extending the scope of the EAD to state level in addition to the regional organization level. By this time, the EAD encompassed most of the European and Arab states in addition to the original initiators, the EC and the League of Arab States. Inclusion of the PLO, and European acceptance of this inclusion, indicated to the Arab side an indirect recognition of the PLO by the Europeans.[37] The elevation of the EAD to the political level meant that the EAD not only represented the two respective regional organizations, but also the individual member states as well.

At the meeting Ambassador Wagner called for the concentration of the EAD on technical matters, while entrusting to the General Committee the task of co-ordination of other EAD activities. He also viewed the EAD as a 'permanent' enterprise, and he did not rule out the possibility of convening a conference at the foreign-minister level if results achieved in the General Committee justified it. While insisting that the EC was interested in developing relations with the 'entire Mediterranean region.', Ambassador Wagner proclaimed: 'the Nine believe that the right of the Palestinian people to the expression of its national identity must be recognized'.[38]

Klaus Meyer, speaking on behalf of the EC Commission, called for common action between the two groups, 'increasing solidarity in all matters of mutual interest for our common economic future'.[39] He argued further that the matter of oil could not remain outside the context of the EAD, since 'an assured and stable access to these traditional sources of supply will continue to be important for the economic health of the Community'. He advised the Arab states to avoid capital-intensive industries, and to concentrate on labour-intensive industries geared for Arab markets rather than for export. He thus anticipated the potential danger of competition resulting from possible future Arab industrial surplus.[40]

The Arabs viewed the EAD as a meeting of two civilizations, and stressed the need for continuity of the EAD. They noted with satisfaction the establishment of PLO information offices in some European capitals, and called on the European countries to halt arms shipments to Israel.

Dr Ahmad Sedki al-Dajani, the representative of the PLO, expressed his satisfaction with the progress of the EAD in defining common ground, but he criticized the Europeans for their adoption of 'a certain style of expression which tends to do its utmost to obscure a clear, undeniable fact', and for their 'hesitancy in dealing with the case of the Palestinian people and calling things by their proper names'.[41]

Second General Committee Meeting in Tunis, 10–12 February 1977

The Luxembourg meeting resulted in some positive financial commitments from the General Council of the League of Arab States. On 9 September 1976 the League budgeted $350,000 for the activities of the EAD.[42] General optimism about the success of the Tunis meeting was also generated by a preliminary European agreement on co-financing the EAD, which was adopted by the EC Council of Ministers in a meeting on 8 February 1977, two days before the Tunis meeting.[43]

The Arab delegation in Tunis, headed by Ambassador Ismael Khalil of Tunisia, assessed the evolution of the EAD and argued that the General Committee had not matched the progress achieved by the other committees. Khalil called upon the Europeans to condemn Israeli disregard of Palestinian human rights and its continued detention of 3,200 Arab political prisoners in subhuman conditions. Khalil challenged the European theory of balance in relations with the Arab states and with Israel, stating that: 'the logic of balance which equates the aggressor with the victim is totally rejected since it allows the occupier to do as he pleases and provides him with the moral support for continuation of his occupation'.[44]

The European delegation, chaired by Ambassador Richard Fiber of Britain, rejected the notion that the EAD should determine European relations with Israel, stressing that: 'the European Community cannot accept that others determine her relations with Israel'.[45] He went on to argue that amicable relations with Israel would enhance EC contributions to a peaceful settlement.

The European delegation went on record at the Tunis meeting as stating their rejection of continued Israeli occupation of Arab lands, the establishment of Israeli settlements in these territories, and unilateral changes in the status of Jerusalem. The Arabs proposed the establishment of a political consultation committee within the EAD, and the Europeans promised to study this proposal.[46]

The General Committee requested the working Committee on financial co-operation to draft a Euro–Arab convention for the protection of investments, and asked the agricultural committee to accelerate work on a feasibility study for the Juba Valley development project in Somalia.[47]

Third General Committee Meeting in Brussels,
26–8 October 1977

The Brussels meeting took place in an atmosphere of optimism. It followed closely the European summit declaration in London on 29 June 1977, which came closer to recognizing the PLO than had any previous European declaration. The London summit communiqué emphasized the need for 'giving effective expression to Palestinian national identity', and identified the importance of 'a homeland for the Palestinians'.[48] The Brussels meeting coincided with European endorsement of UN Resolution 126 (27 October 1977), which called upon Israel to abandon its illegal annexation of East Jerusalem.[49]

In Brussels, the two sides agreed to respect the sovereignty of Lebanon as a unified state, which in essence meant a call to outside powers to refrain from alliances with warring factions in the civil wars. The Arabs announced their readiness to finance the projects of the EAD to the amount of $15 million. The Europeans committed $3.5 million for the proposed feasibility studies. A list of projects and activities suggested and agreed upon, along with their estimated costs and the contributions of each group, are shown in Table 4.2.[50]

The Effect on the EAD of the Egyptian–Israeli Talks

President Sadat's trip to Israel in November 1977 created an uproar in the Arab world and resulted in the adoption of wide-ranging sanctions against Egypt as a result of the Baghdad Arab summit. Delegates to the summit meeting acted to suspend Egypt's membership of the League of Arab States, to remove the League secretariat from Cairo and transfer it to Tunis, and to provide full financial support to Syria and Jordan, the two other Arab states bordering Israel.

Unlike most of the Arab states, the Europeans welcomed the 'courageous' actions of President Sadat and were very optimistic about an eventual agreement between Egypt and Israel. Both groups were eagerly awaiting the outcome of Sadat's visit and the efforts of US President Jimmy Carter, who had been working since the beginning of the year to bring about an agreement between Israel and Egypt. American diplomatic

Table 4.2. Budgeting of Euro–Arab Dialogue Activities, Third General Committee Meeting, Brussels, 26–28 October 1977 (US dollars)

	Estimated cost	Estimated Contributions	
		Arab	European
Symposium on relations between the two civilizations	250,000	125,000	125,000
Basic infrastructure			
Training programme in maritime transport	200,000	160,000	40,000
Harmonization of statistics in Arab ports	60,000	48,000	12,000
Study for development of a new port at al-Basrah, Iraq	500,000	400,000	100,000
Study for development of a port at Tartus, Syria	500,000	400,000	100,000
Symposium on the theme of 'new cities'	20,000	10,000	10,000
Agriculture and rural development			
The Juba Valley: a study of an irrigation project at Bardera, Somalia	1,200,000	960,000	240,000
Sudan meat production project	50,000	40,000	10,000
Project for growing seed potatoes in Iraq	1,800,000	1,440,000	360,000

Source: Euro–Arab Dialogue, General Committee, 'Final Communiqué', Brussels, 26–8 October 1977 (Brussels, Commission of the European Communities), Annex, p. 18.

activities in the area consequently meant a diminution of the role of the Europeans. As a result of this combination of factors the planned general meeting of the EAD, which had been scheduled to be held in Khartoum, Sudan in early 1978, was postponed until the end of 1978.

In light of these developments it took extraordinary determination on the part of the European and Arab members of the EAD at the expert level to keep it functioning during the turbulent year of 1978 and to make a general meeting possible by December 1978.

Fourth General Committee Meeting in Damascus,
9–11 December 1978

The Damascus meeting was more functional than political. The delegates reviewed the progress of the work of the different committees and offered some new guidelines for the specialized committees. Politically, both sides reiterated their support for continuation of the EAD. The delegates also passed a resolution in which they committed their respective countries once again to the continued independence and sovereignty of Lebanon.

The General Committee called on the experts to consider vocational training as a priority item on their agenda. It also approved the establishment of a Euro–Arab centre for the transfer of technology, and agreed on possible inputs from the specialized committee on trade on the subject of a trade convention. The Arabs advocated a preferential arrangement, since exports of Kuwaiti urea and Tunisian textiles were encountering difficulties in the EC tariff system. The Europeans, in turn, insisted on a reciprocal arrangement. However, the two sides agreed on the preliminary financing of a few projects and adopted a joint declaration on the principles governing living and working conditions of guest workers in both regions, with equal-treatment clauses regarding working conditions, wages, and economic rights. (See Table 4.3.)

The Impact of the Camp David Agreement

The signing of the Camp David agreement between Egypt and Israel in September 1978 sent shock waves through the Arab world and Europe. As a result, Egypt became estranged from the rest of the Arab world, and the ideals of Arab nationalism and the *raison d'être* for the League of Arab States were shaken.

The divergence of Arab and European views over the Camp David agreement and other procedural problems involved with moving the secretariat of the League of Arab States from Cairo to new headquarters in Tunis resulted in a suspension of the EAD for a period of more than twenty months. The Arabs were alerted to rumours emanating from Brussels regarding the possibility of the Europeans dealing with two Arab League secretariats, one in Tunis and another in Cairo. Also, the EC had stated its reluctance to deal with the Arab League without the inclusion of Egypt, whose peace policies it supported reservedly. The Arabs, on their part, insisted that the EC should be engaged in relations with the League of Arab States and its member countries, and since Egypt's membership of the League had been suspended the EC could not expect Egypt to be a participant in the EAD. At a later stage of the

Table 4.3. Studies and Activities Considered by the Fourth General
Committee Meeting of the Euro–Arab Dialogue in
Damascus, 9–11 December 1978 (US dollars)

Studies and other activities	Estimated total costs	Contributions	
		Arab	European
Industrialization			
Setting up of Euro–Arab documentation and information centres for standardization	450,000	360,000	90,000
Study on petrochemical industries	165,000	132,000	33,000
Study on oil-refining industries	165,000	132,000	33,000
Study on policies and programmes for education and training in fields of standardization, metrology, and quality control	135,000	108,000	27,000
Cultural and social questions			
Publication of proceedings of the Venice seminar on 'Means and Forms of Co-operation for the Dissemination in Europe of Knowledge of the Arab Language and Literary Civilization'.	20,000	10,000	10,000
Draft catalogue of cultural and scientific institutions	6,000	3,000	3,000
Technical assistance for the establishment of an Arab vocational and instructor training centre	880,000	704,000	176,000
Scientific and technical co-operation			
Study for the establishment of an Arab institute for water desalinization and resources	600,000	480,000	120,000
Feasibility study for the establishment of an Arab polytechnic institute	1,000,000	800,000	200,000
Survey of scientific infrastructure on marine science in the Arab countries	160,000	128,000	32,000
Additional amount for the Hampburg symposium on the relationship between the two civilizations	115,000	57,500	57,500
Total	3,696,000	2,914,500	781,500

Source: Euro–Arab Dialogue, General Committee, 'Final Communiqué', Damascus, 9–11 December 1978 (Cairo, League of Arab States).

negotiations between the two sides an agreement was reached whereby Egypt, while not participating in the EAD negotiations, would be continuously informed by the Europeans of developments in the dialogue.[51]

In March 1980 the Arab League agreed to renew preliminary contact with the Europeans. Such contact resumed. Chadli Kalibi, the new secretary-general of the League of Arab States, met with Gaston Thorn (the Foreign Minister of Luxembourg and president of the European Council) on 22 July 1980 in Brussels, and the two agreed that the EAD would be resumed at the preliminary level.[52] Preliminary meetings were held in Tunis on 30 July and 18 October 1980. These two meetings resulted in an agreement to call for a meeting of the General Committee to be held on 12–13 November 1980, at the ambassadorial level.[53]

Fifth General Committee Meeting in Luxembourg, 12–13 November 1980

This meeting was held on a trilateral level. The European side was chaired by Paul Helmunger, Luxembourg Secretary of State for Foreign Affairs and president of the EC Council of Ministers, by Claude Cheysson, EC development commissioner, and by representatives of past and future presidents of the EC Council of Ministers. The Arab side was chaired by Dr Ahmad Sedki al-Dajani of the PLO, representing the League of Arab States, assisted by Adnan Omran, assistant secretary-general of the League, and by representatives of Oman and Qatar. This trilateral representation on both sides was an attempt to give continuity to the work of the General Committee as well as an attempt by the EC to avoid *de facto* recognition of the PLO, since it was, in effect, talking to the Arab League as a whole.[54]

At the Luxembourg meeting the two sides agreed to hold an EAD meeting at the foreign-minister level in June or July 1981. However, later developments, which were the result of a change of government in France, resulted in postponement of this meeting until autumn 1981. The two groups agreed, at the Luxembourg meeting, on the 'comprehensive and permanent nature of the dialogue', and called upon the specialized committees to accelerate work on a number of projects such as the proposed convention on the promotion and protection of investments.[55]

Salient Points of the EAD

In its five years of existence the Euro–Arab Dialogue has succeeded in bridging the gap in political views between the two sides. As a novel inter-regional experiment, the EAD contributed to allaying mutual fears and misconceptions. In 1975, Arabs and Europeans were sitting together mutually searching for common ways to enhance their political and functional co-operation. This in itself is a dramatic achievement, given that only two decades earlier the whole of the Arab region was an appendage to Europe.

Despite periodic evaluations, delays, and suspensions the EAD became a permanent instrument for direct interaction and exchange. Even during the uncertain period of 1978 the functional committees continued to meet fairly regularly. Except for 1977, the most active year for the EAD, the General Committee met only once a year. However, the EAD remained an effective means of information-gathering for the two regions and for their regional organizations, the League of Arab States and the EC.

Meetings at the functional, or expert, level were far more successful than were those at the political level. The economic development of the Arab regions gave the EAD credibility. There were few disagreements between the two sides on the means. The Europeans sought to maximize the participation of European corporations in the expanding construction markets in the Arab world. There is, however, no specific way to determine whether or not that objective has been helped or accelerated by the EAD.

Both European and Arab parties were interested in agricultural and rural development. Many studies on regional development projects, such as those in the Sudan, Somalia, and Syria, were discussed in detail. The function of the EAD has been to give visibility to the need for such projects—though not to finance them, beyond possibly the financing of feasibility studies. The EAD has neither the funds nor the personnel to undertake such a massive enterprise. However, both groups have been aware that the EAD could bring the need for such projects to the attention of other regional organizations in Europe and the Arab world which could, perhaps, undertake the financing of them.

The Europeans, overall, have preferred that financing of individual projects be carried out by the private sector. Government budget constraints were given as the reason for this, but both sides expressed their commitment to the success of the EAD through a commitment of $15 million by the Arabs and $3.5 million by the Europeans.

Specific economic achievements by the EAD have not been major.

As a reflection of the concern of the Mahgreb countries over the living and working conditions of their citizens working in Europe, on 11 December 1978 at Damascus the EAD adopted a joint declaration on the principles concerning the living and working conditions of migrant labour in the two regions. The fourteen-point declaration stressed the economic equality of migrant workers with the citizens of the host countries, legal representation of the workers, and vocational education for the workers and their children.

Arab countries with financial surplus to invest, have consistently worked within the EAD for an intra-regional investment convention which would guarantee protection from non-financial injuries for the investments of their nationals and their companies. The draft agreement between the EC and the League of Arab States calls for providing most-favoured-nation treatment to the investments and companies of the respective member states. It also guarantees freedom of movement of capital and allows the host country to restrict this transfer of capital only for non-discriminatory purposes of balance of payments problems or as a reaction to collective withdrawal of funds. The proposed agreement would also insure prospective foreign investors against non-economic injuries to property arising from a *coup d'état* or violent public action. It would provide for a collective fund established by concerned countries which would act as an insuring corporation. Article 18 of the proposed convention provides for a four-level method of settlement of disputes, ranging from diplomatic contacts to conciliation, arbitration, court action, or the adjudication of difficult cases by the International Centre for the Settlement of Disputes, an organization within the World Bank.[56]

Another project which should also be ready for ratification by the EAD General Committee is the proposed Euro–Arab centre for technology transfer, which is to be established in Kuwait.

In terms of political accomplishments, the EAD has succeeded in modifying somewhat the public policies of certain European countries. British and German foreign policies, which have traditionally been sensitive to changes in the political barometer in Washington, have clearly of late been following a policy critical of Israel's establishment of new settlements in occupied Arab territories. Their voting patterns in the UN have reflected this change. Whereas in 1974, Britain, Holland, and Denmark voted against the UN proposal to invite the PLO to participate as an observer, and France, Italy, and Ireland voted for that resolution, all of the EC countries have subsequently supported UN resolutions calling on Israel to abandon its policies with regard to settlements in occupied Arab territories.[57]

However, neither the EAD efforts, or other diplomatic efforts managed by the PLO, have brought about *de jure* recognition by the Europeans of the PLO as the sole representative of the Palestinian people. The PLO, however, has successfully utilized the aegis of the EAD to further its diplomatic status in Europe, a subject which will be analysed in Chapter 7. Suffice it to mention here that the basic objective of the Arabs in the EAD was frustrated by many factors and pressures, both internal and external. The PLO, which is recognized by more than a hundred nations in the world, has historically had great difficulty in favourably impressing public opinion in the Western nations.

The Europeans, for their part, failed to secure through the EAD an assured petroleum supply from the Arab world. This goal had been a constant motivating force behind European acceptance of the EAD.

A disinterested observer would conclude that the EAD has reflected European concern over energy supplies and Arab concern over Western European recognition of the PLO. These two imperatives explain the reactivation of the EAD in the autumn of 1980, after a cessation of nearly two years. The

Europeans were worried about declining oil production in Iran, and the Arabs were concerned by the separate peace treaty signed between Egypt and Israel.

The EAD has succeeded in preserving the spirit of regional co-operation in both communities. Arab nationalists saw in the EAD a force for collective diplomatic Arab action that tended to mediate internal Arab differences. Similarly, the EAD helped to foster a growth of European solidarity and co-operation between the EPCS and the EC, since the latter was entrusted with collaboration in negotiating the technical issues of the EAD.

Problems of the EAD

The professed goal of the Euro–Arab Dialogue has been to expand areas of co-operation between the Arab world and Europe. The EAD has provided some ten or twelve studies on various development projects. It has also established a permanent mechanism for an exchange of views between the two sides. However, initial optimism has proved to be somewhat unfounded. Europe has not proved to be a credible 'third alternative' for effecting a peaceful resolution of the Arab–Israeli conflict, nor has it been the method for assuring the Europeans of a steady and continuous supply of Arab oil. On all of these counts, bilateral agreements between individual Arab countries and individual European countries have proved to be more effective. It is fitting, therefore, that each act of co-operation within the EAD has been based largely on existing bilateral agreements.[58]

The EAD has, however, demonstrated a certain resilience. A community of interest has developed between the Arabs and the Europeans, especially between high-ranking bureaucrats in the League of Arab States and the EC. The EAD has been a major interest of Chadli Kalibi, secretary-general of the League of Arab States. He organized a special unit for the EAD that is attached directly to his office, and members of that unit engage in a certain amount of lobbying within the League. Similarly, in Europe, members of the Commission's Development Directorate are responsible for the EAD work on its behalf.

In evaluating the EAD, author Alan Taylor feels that a divergence of attitudes among the European countries with regard to the Arab–Israeli conflict has proved to be an obstacle for the dialogue. He points out that some of the Arab countries, such as Egypt, have supported a certain degree of co-ordination between the US and Europe with regard to declarations on Middle East questions, but that other Arab countries and France, during the presidency of Valéry Giscard d'Estaing, have advocated independence from US diplomatic activities.[59]

The US has influenced developments within the EAD. At Abu Dhabi (21 November 1975), it was instrumental in keeping oil matters outside the scope of the EAD. Its attitudes have affected the political position of some EC countries, such as the German position on the PLO at the Venice summit meeting of June 1980. Active US involvement in the Arab region has militated against conducting political discussions within the EAD, such as during the period 1978–9. US concern with the EAD will be discussed in more detail in a subsequent chapter.

Progress within the EAD has been hindered to some extent by the structures of some of the participating governments. The Arab League, for example, represents countries with a myriad of political systems—monarchies, socialist republics, and others. The common denominator for all of these countries is that the government plays an active role in the national economy. The EC countries, by contrast, operate within a free-market system in which the most prominent roles are played by those in the private sector. These divergent government/economic points of view should not, however, preclude measurable co-operation. For example, Arab agencies have successfully collaborated in the past with a number of foreign private concerns in joint ventures.[60]

Through the EAD the Europeans may have sought to affect the economic development of the Arab region to forestall possible future competition from Arab producers of petrochemicals who have advantages over their European counterparts. The EC, however, seems to have recognized the need for progressive adaptation to changing patterns of international trade. European political leaders have come to recognize the desirability of Arab and African industrialization as a means of ensuring a stable political milieu in these countries.

The EAD as a form of Associative Diplomacy

The EAD was organized in the aftermath of the 1973 Arab–Israeli war as a means of presenting the Arab world, as a single entity, to the EC. The Europeans recognized the need for such a linkage because of their need for oil and raw materials. Historically, the prices of these commodities have been the major concern of industrialized countries. However, after the war more basic questions of continued adequate supplies and information pertaining to planned production became paramount. The Arabs needed diplomatic allies wherever they could be found. Europe also had a special appeal to the Arab countries. It had been the economic and political model for the Arabs, and its perceived influence on US foreign policy made alliance even more appealing.

Arab diplomatic efforts in 1974 and 1975 were aimed at the elevation of the PLO to the status of representative of a state in exile, and at its inclusion in negotiations on any matters pertaining to the Middle East. Despite the failure of the EAD to result in recognition of the PLO the latter was, nevertheless, one of the most active supporters of the EAD. The PLO may have wanted to use the EAD as a channel for airing its demands, and in this regard it may have been successful.

Although falling short of achieving formal recognition for the PLO the EAD did, however, succeed in persuading the Europeans of the need to establish a 'homeland for the Palestinians', and in 'associating' the PLO with future negotiations on the Middle East. Thus, the EAD has served certain limited Arab objectives.

In associating themselves with the Arab world through the EAD the EPCS and the EC have created a climate favourable to independent European action. The resilience of the EAD has also been due to the gradual involvement of the smaller European countries who initially were hesitant about joining the dialogue, but found that active involvement in EAD discussions provided them with considerable benefits at the bilateral level. A case in point is Belgium, which seems to have been able to secure major construction contracts in Saudi Arabia and other Gulf states, due in large part to its hosting of several EAD meetings in 1976.

Notes

1. Some news reports have quoted the former US Secretary of State Henry Kissinger as having expressed 'disgust' over the neutral stand of the NATO countries in the 1973 Middle East war; see the *Washington Post* (1 November 1973), p. 12.
2. A letter sent to the UN secretary-general by Otto Borch, Danish representative to the UN, on behalf of the European Political Co-operation System (EPCS) informing him of the decisions of the foreign ministers is included in the Appendix in A. S. al-Dajani, *Al Hiwar al-Arabi el-Urubbi, Wijhat Nazar Arabiyah wah-Wathaiq* [The Euro–Arab Dialogue: An Arab Viewpoint and Documents] (Beirut and Cairo, Anglo-Egyptian Library, 1976, in Arabic), pp. 171-3.
3. See the Arab summit resolution, ibid., pp. 174-5.
4. I am grateful to Professor Susan Strange for her insight in this regard.
5. *Washington Post* (30 November 1973), p. 30.
6. See the text of the EC Council of Ministers' proposal in *The New York Times* (5 March 1974), p. 6.
7. *Bulletin of the European Communities*, 6/3 (1973), p. 10.
8. See Mr Riad's speech at the first General Committee meeting in Luxembourg on 18-20 May 1976, in Euro–Arab Dialogue, *First General Meeting of the Euro–Arab Dialogue* (Cairo, League of Arab States, 1976), p. 37.
9. The two conferences are noted in al-Dajani, op. cit., pp. 5-6.
10. For a full review of the Milan conference, see *Lo Spettatore Internazionale* (English edn: *The International Observer*), 9/2 (April–June 1974).
11. Ibid., p. 83.
12. Ibid., p. 82.
13. See resolution adopted in Damascus (14–17 September 1974) and a list of participants, in *Documents de la 1er Conference Interparlementaire Preparatoire pour la Cooperation Euro–Arab* [Documents of the First Interparliamentary Conference Preparatory to Euro–Arab Co-operation] (Damascus, Office de Presse et Documentation (OFA), Dialogue Euro-Arabe, 1974, in French).
14. Personal correspondence with Mr Robert Swann, secretary of the Parliamentary Association for Euro–Arab Co-operation, 20 August 1980.
15. A. Taylor, *The Euro–Arab Dialogue* (Middle East Problem Paper No. 15, Washington DC, The Middle East Institute, April 1978), p. 2.
16. Yusuf Sayigh, 'Defense of the Oil-Producing Arab Countries', *Lo Spettatore Internazionale* (English edn: *The International Observer*), 9/2 (April–June 1974), 97-101.
17. Taylor, op. cit., p. 7.

18. See Euro-Arab Dialogue, 'Joint Memorandum', Cairo, 14 June 1975 (Brussels, Commission of the European Communities), p. 5.

19. The subject of the importance of the European private sector's input for the success of the EAD is restated in speeches of the EC Commission delegates at the various meetings of the EAD. See, for example, the speech of Dr Klaus Meyer, deputy secretary-general of the EC Commission in Tunis, in L'Ambassade du Tunisie au Caire, *The Euro-Arab Dialogue, First General Committee Meeting, Luxembourg 18-20 May 1976* (Cairo, 1976), p. 6.

20. See the speech of Claude Cheysson at the Damascus meeting of the EAD in Euro-Arab Dialogue, General Committee, 'Final Communiqué', Damascus, 9-11 December 1978 (Cairo, League of Arab States).

21. Personal interviews in Brussels and Tunis, November and December 1980.

22. The thirty-one members of the Euro-Arab Dialogue are: Algeria, Morocco, Tunisia, Mauritania, Libya, Egypt, Sudan, Somalia, Jibuti, Palestine, Lebanon, Syria, Iraq, Kuwait, Bahrain, the United Arab Emirates, Qatar, Oman, Saudi Arabia, North Yemen, South Yemen, France, Britain, West Germany, Italy, Greece, the Netherlands, Belgium, Denmark, Luxembourg, and the Republic of Ireland.

23. *The New York Times* (30 April 1981), p. 6.

24. Based on interviews at the secretariat of League of Arab States, Tunis, December 1980.

25. Interviews in Brussels at the offices of the EC, 21 November 1980.

26. Ibid.

27. See Euro-Arab Dialogue, 'Joint Memorandum', cited in Note 18, p. 1.

28. See Palestine Liberation Organization, 'Report to the Secretariat of the League of Arab States, 8 August 1976', in A. al-Dajani, *The Palestine Liberation Organization and the Euro-Arab Dialogue: A Study of the Political Aspects of the Dialogue and Documents* (Beirut, PLO Research Centre, 1976, in Arabic), p. 123. See also *The New York Times* (5 and 13 March 1975).

29. Euro-Arab Dialogue, 'Joint Memorandum', cited in Note 18, pp. 2-3.

30. Euro-Arab Dialogue and Commission of the European Communities, 'Joint Working Paper', Rome, 24 July 1975 (Brussels, Commission of the European Communities), p. 7.

31. Arab concerns were heightened by the US Senate hearings on foreign commerce and tourism of the Committee on Commerce, US Senate, 7 and 12 May 1975 (Washington DC, Government Printing Office, 1975).

32. Euro-Arab Dialogue and Commission of the European Communities, 'Joint Working Paper', cited in Note 30.

33. This information was derived from personal interviews with EC officials in Brussels, 21 November 1980.

34. Euro–Arab Dialogue and League of Arab States, 'Joint Working Paper', Abu Dhabi, 27 November 1975 (Cairo, League of Arab States), p. 2.
35. Ibid., p. 42.
36. Ibid., p. 6.
37. See the speech of Ambassador al-Shamlan in L'Ambassade du Tunisie au Caire, op. cit., p. 27.
38. Ibid., p. 10.
39. Ibid., p. 15.
40. Ibid., p. 17.
41. Ibid., p. 55.
42. A verbatim copy of the General Council's decision is included in al-Dajani, *The Palestine Liberation Organization and the Euro–Arab Dialogue*, cited in Note 28, p. 127.
43. *Bulletin of the European Communities*, 10/1 (1977), p. 62.
44. al-Dajani, *The Palestine Liberation Organization and the Euro–Arab Dialogue*, cited in Note 28, p. 138.
45. Ibid., p. 147.
46. Euro–Arab Dialogue, General Committee, 'Final Communiqué', Tunis, 10–12 February 1977 (Cairo, League of Arab States), p. 3.
47. Ibid., p. 9.
48. *Bulletin of the European Communities*, 10/6 (1977), p. 62.
49. U. Steinbach, 'Western European and EC Policies Toward Mediterranean and Middle Eastern Countries', in C. Legum *et al., Middle East Contemporary Survey, Vol. II (1977–78)* (New York and London, Holmes and Meier, 1979), p. 45.
50. Euro–Arab Dialogue, General Committee, 'Final Communiqué', Brussels, 26–8 October 1977 (Brussels, Commission of the European Communities), p. 18.
51. *Europe Political Day* (Agence Internationale d'Information pour la Presse, Luxembourg-Brussels) 2954 (22–3 July 1980).
52. League of Arab States, internal memorandums of 2 September and 18 October 1980.
53. At a dinner hosted by Dr al-Dajani, the Palestine Liberation Organization executive committee members, and chairmen of the Arab delegations to the Luxembourg meeting. al-Dajani issued his invitation to the European delegation in the name of the Palestine Liberation Organization, not the Arab League. The fact that most senior European participants attended the PLO-hosted dinner gave the Arab delegation further proof of a *de facto* recognition of the PLO by the EC.
54. Euro–Arab Dialogue, 'Joint Communiqué', Luxembourg, 12–13 November 1980 (Brussels, Commission of the European Communities).

55. League of Arab States, Secretariat-General, Department of Economic Affairs, 'Draft Agreement between Member Countries of the League of Arab States and Member Countries of the European Economic Community on the Mutual Promotion and Protection of Respective Investments' (Tunis, 1980).
56. Chapter 5 of this book includes detailed discussions of this draft agreement.
57. Based on the author's review of UN General Assembly resolutions on the Middle East for the period 1974–80.
58. Taylor, op. cit., p. 5.
59. Ibid., p. 9.
60. Such successful co-operation between the Arab states and the multi-national corporations is a direct refutation of Alan Taylor's thesis, as stated in Taylor, op. cit., p. 8.

5 THE BILATERAL AGREEMENTS

At the time of its inception in 1957, the European Community (EC) incorporated special arrangements whereby non-European states and territories were to be included in the Common Market through co-operation agreements, or association. These agreements were aimed at providing preferential trade export possibilities and other economic benefits to the parties, and also provided for aid for economic and social development in the emerging nations.[1]

In 1957, at the time of the signing of the Treaty of Rome by which the EC was formally established, vast African territories were connected to EC member states, particularly France and Belgium. After 1960 most of these territories had gained their independence, and these special arrangements evolved into a series of bilateral trade agreements between the EC and the individual emerging states such as Algeria, Morocco, and Tunisia.

Although these association agreements were ultimately concluded with a number of countries[2] (European associated states such as Spain and Greece could and did qualify for full membership), a detailed examination here of the trade agreements between the EC and three of the North African Mahgreb countries—Tunisia, Morocco, and Algeria—will be discussed in some detail as examples of bilateral agreements which furthered regional dependence.

It should be noted here that although the Arab Mahgreb countries participated actively in the first phase of the EC's association system, the Arab Mashreq countries, with the exception of Lebanon, were cool toward such a plan and viewed it as a form of 'neo-colonialism'. The Mashreq countries also feared that a preferential trade agreement with Israel might weaken the Arab boycott of Israeli goods and services.[3] It was not until 1968 that the League of Arab States changed its position and encouraged its member states to negotiate trade agreements with the EC.[4]

The Early Phase of the Association Agreements

The EC's association system, even at the beginning, differentiated between various countries or groups of countries. As has been noted, European associated states were viewed as eligible for future full participation in the EC, with the association phase serving as an intermediate phase. African associated states, such as the Yaoundé group, were seen to benefit from preferential access to European markets and were considered eligible for European aid commitments. The Mahgreb countries were accorded special association in the form of trade agreements, but did not initially receive any significant aid commitments. Other Middle Eastern countries, such as Egypt and Israel, were also linked to the EC by preferential trade agreements.

Within this hierarchy, the EC signed preferential trade agreements with Lebanon and Israel in 1964 and special association agreements with Tunisia and Morocco in 1969. Attempts by Algeria to negotiate a similar agreement were unsuccessful, since Algeria had already signed a fifteen-year oil agreement with France in 1965 which guaranteed some concessions for French companies in the Sahara and included provisions for the access of Algerian products to French markets. Algeria had also negotiated a trade agreement with the Federal Republic of Germany in 1966, providing for a 10 per cent tariff reduction on its wines.[5]

The Global Mediterranean Policy

In 1972 the EC Executive Commission was asked by the EC Council of Ministers to 'submit firm proposals for a global approach to all the Community relations with the Mediterranean countries',[6] as well as to consider the effect of the impending entry of Denmark, Great Britain, and Ireland on EC relations with the southern Mediterranean countries.

The Commission drew up a paper in which it emphasized the need to aid in the economic development of these countries through the expansion of their industrial exports to the EC, with the optimistic objective of removing most barriers to industrial trade by 1 July 1977. The Commission also acknowledged that the Community's Common Agricultural

Policy (CAP) tended to inhibit agricultural trade with the Mediterranean countries and called for 'suitable concessions to be granted without endangering the legitimate interests of member states'.[7] Such a policy was debated in the EC Council of Ministers in the autumn of 1972 and adopted at the Paris summit meeting of 19–20 October 1972.

While encompassing both Arab and non-Arab states in the Mediterranean basin, the policy reflected the 'desire of the Nine to develop balanced economic relations with the Mediterranean coastal states in this particularly "sensitive" area of the world'.[8] Bilateral agreements were concluded with seven Arab countries in North Africa and West Asia (Figure 5.1), in addition to Israel

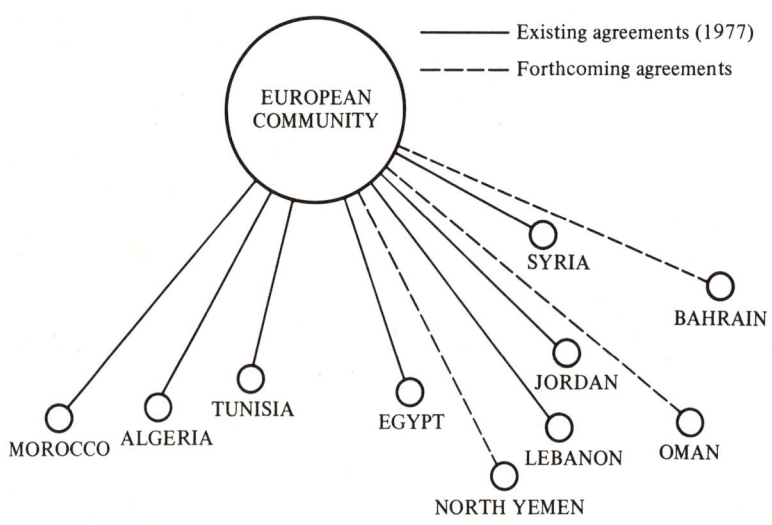

Fig. 5.1. European Community Bilateral Co-operation Agreements with the Arab States, 1977.

and other European Mediterranean states. The bilateral agreements sought to establish commercial and technical co-operation with the seven Arab states as well as to provide them with some form of development assistance amounting to 632 million EUA (European Units of Account). This amounted to 293 million EUA ($300 million) over five years (1977–81) directed to the

Table 5.1. European Community Financial Co-operation with
Mahgreb* and Mashreq† Countries (1977–1981)‡

Form of aid	Amount per country (in million EUA)						
	Algeria	Morocco	Tunisia	Egypt	Jordan	Syria	Lebanon
Normal EIB loans	70	56	41	93	18	34	20
Special loans	19	58	39	14	4	7	2
Grants	25	16	15	63	18	12	8
TOTAL	114	130	95	170	40	53	30

*Algeria, Morocco, Tunisia.
†West Asia Arab countries.
‡Excluding food aid from the EC to these countries.
Source: European Community Commission, *The European Community and the Third World* (Brussels, November 1977), p. 30.

four Mashreq countries, and 339 million EUA ($376 million) to the three Mahgreb countries (Table 5.1).

This policy reflected the liberal views of the EC at the time, since it projected the establishment of a free-trade area in the Mediterranean centred around the EC. Political and commercial motives may have furthered the development of such a policy. The trade imperative of the area may not have been a high priority for the EC at that time, since it accounted for only 3.7 per cent of total EC exports. However, when the expansion of EC trade with the Arab world as a whole is viewed, it accounted for 15 per cent of extra-EC exports in 1979, and when the precursory nature of the Mahgreb and Mashreq agreements is considered we begin to see the potential impact of these agreements on the wider EC market in the Arab oil-producing countries. That is to say, although the overall importance of the Mahgreb and Mashreq markets for the EC was minimal, it did not escape the attention of the Community's planners that such an organization of the export–import market could form the basis for a subsequent and significant trade bloc encompassing all of the Arab League states.[9]

It is also important to recognize the significance of the EC markets to the Mashreq and Mahgreb countries. For example, Morocco directs nearly 59 per cent of its total exports to the EC. The imbalance between the perceived commercial needs of the EC and the Mahgreb and Mashreq countries may have been recognized by the Arabs, and may even have prevented the Arab negotiators from attempting to seek more favourable agreements for agricultural products, as in the case of Algerian wine.

What then are the essential political factors behind the EC's Mediterranean policy? In reading the preambles to these agreements, one discerns a genuine interest on the part of the EC in the economic development of the region. Public opinion polls taken in the EC at the time support such a stance,[10] and the views of European élites also strongly reflected this special attachment.[11] European anxiety over the security of oil lines may also have encouraged support for the economic development of the area, since such development was viewed as a prerequisite for political stability. Whether the EC viewed the Mediterranean as *'Mare nostrum'*, as Werner Feld would have us believe, or as a future trading bloc, as the actual growth of Euro–Arab trade indicates (the Arab world is the largest EC trade partner), the policy remains politically motivated. It should not be surprising that any EC political policy is clothed in trade cloaks, for most European attempts at political unification have traditionally taken a functional garb.

The General Characteristics of the EC Bilateral Agreements

Contrary to the EC Commission's claim that the bilateral agreements with the Arab Mediterranean countries were tailored specifically to the particular needs of each country, there is more similarity between these parallel co-operation agreements than there are differences.[12]

The agreements signed in 1976 and 1977 with the seven Arab countries of Morocco, Algeria, Tunisia, Egypt, Syria, Lebanon, and Jordan, share the following attributes:

(1) Trade provisions that are aimed at allowing free entry of most Arab industrial products, bar those labelled as 'sensitive', and other agricultural products. (In the case of Algeria, sensitive industrial products include cork and cork products as well as refined petroleum, a product universally defined as 'sensitive'.)
(2) Certain import regimes are stated for processed agricultural products such as refined olive oil.

(3) A tariff concession is granted on some agricultural products covered by the CAP, provided that these products abide by a single or multiple application of 'safeguard clauses' such as certain import calendars, reference prices, and/or export taxes on the product collected prior to its shipment by the Mediterranean country concerned.[13] (The purpose of these import calanders is to provide European consumers with southern Mediterranean produce in the off-season. Moroccan vegetables, such as tomatoes, are allowed a 60 per cent tariff reduction if they reach a European port between 1 November and 30 April. Similarly, canned citrus products are allowed entry at 80 per cent of the normal duty if the total weight of the can and contents is 1-kilogram or less (depending upon sugar-added content).)

(4) In every bilateral agreement, especially for the Mahgreb countries, there is a section (which had probably involved considerable negotiation) delineating the import regime of key farm products—olive oil in Tunisia, wine in Algeria, and citrus fruit and tinned sardines in Morocco.

(5) Every agreement also includes a 'definition of an originating product', which specifies that a product designated as such and benefiting from the tariff reduction must be 'wholly obtained' and/or 'sufficiently processed' inside the given country. In the case of the Mahgreb countries, the three states are considered as a single zone.

(6) Every bilateral agreement contains a clause granting the EC most-favoured-nation status which, although it does not require the Mahgreb countries to reciprocate the EC reductions (in contrast to Egypt and Lebanon), it does commit these countries to 'extend to the Nine any favourable trading terms offered in subsequent agreements with other countries'.[14]

(7) An economic and technical co-operation measure is included, with promises of help in economic planning, and in business and scientific co-operation.

(8) A financial aid programme is included, ranging from 170 million EUA to Egypt to 30 million EUA to Lebanon over the five years (1977–81). (See Table 5.1.)

Unlike the agreements with the Mashreq countries, those with the Mahgreb countries contain a very progressive labour code covering approximately 800,000 Mahgreb migrant workers in EC countries. The code is similar to the declaration adopted by the Euro–Arab Dialogue at the Damascus meeting of 9–11 December 1978 and calls for, among other things, the 'additionality' of periods of insurance and employment for social security benefits.

Each of these parallel bilateral agreements is of unlimited duration, open for revision first in 1978–9 and every five years thereafter. Each agreement is supervised by a co-operation council, usually at ministerial level, assisted by a lower-level co-operation committee and a specialist committee.

The agreements are open for modification in view of balance of payments problems and/or in case of the adoption of comprehensive policies by the EC, such as a commerical or energy policies.

Problems and Obstacles in EC Trade with the Arab Mediterranean Countries

Despite the fact that the EC is the largest market for southern Mediterranean products, the bilateral agreements have not produced a fully integrated market between the EC and its southern partners. The EC's optimistic prediction of the removal of all trade barriers by 1979 was not achieved due to a number of factors, some less obvious than others.[15]

Since the EC maintains a comprehensive structure of farm subsidies and artificial prices for sugar and other products, the CAP takes precedence over any EC political efforts, even those of associative diplomacy. Member states such as Italy and France have traditionally been critical of the EC's liberal attitudes to giving Third World Countries better access to Community markets. Italian and French concerns are well founded in this regard, since these two countries often find themselves in direct competition with Mahgreb products. Italy and France are the major destinations within the EC for Mahgreb products.[16]

An Italian memorandum of 1964 sought to establish the principle of compensatory payment to member states to make up for losses arising from competition with the associated states. Such a principle, while it proved unacceptable to the other member states, nevertheless led the EC to formulate a major internal, or regional, policy to even out economic and technological differences between European regions.

Italy's concern was again voiced in the European Parliament and, on 11 January 1978, three parliamentary committees commissioned a major study on 'the effects of the Mediterranean policy on Community agriculture'. The report reflected uneasiness over the Commission's Third World policy and called for an expansion of the umbrella support system to other Mediterranean products, such as lamb or mutton and potatoes.[17]

Although the policy statements of the EC Commission are more liberal than those of the European Parliament, the Commission's application of agreements with the southern and eastern Mediterranean countries appears to be limited and cautious. As is shown in Table 5.2, Mahgreb exports suffered

Table 5.2. Index of the Increase in the Value of European Community Imports from Arab Mahgreb and Mashreq Countries, 1972–1979 (1972 = 100)

Country	1972	1973	1974	1975	1976	1977	1978	1979
Algeria	100	152	291	291	278	275	295	442
Morocco	100	145	206	206	193	197	223	290
Tunisia	100	109	234	204	212	301	341	507
Mahgreb average	100	135.3	249.3	233.6	227.6	257.6	286.3	413
Egypt	100	149	212	256	479	511	791	1,250
Jordan*	–	–	–	–	–	–	–	–
Lebanon	100	172	297	84	53	49	46	66
Syria	100	157	387	662	840	795	746	967
Mashreq average	100	159.3	298.6	334	458.3	451	528	761

*EC imports from Jordan are insignificant.

Source: International Monetary Fund, *Direction of Trade Statistics Annual* (Washington DC, IMF, issues 1973–80).

considerably in 1975 and 1976 as a result of an intricate web of import ceilings, or quotas, on textiles, refined petroleum products, and wine. Thus, even though the Community is theoretically committed to allowing the free entry of southern Mediterranean industrial goods to EC markets, such entry is in fact very selected, and is at times extremely restricted.

A case in point is Algerian wine. The negotiated agreement between the EC and Algeria provides for a five-year programme in which the quality of Algerian wine is emphasized and the size of EC imports of this wine increases progressively, at the expense of the so-called bulk wine.[18] Algeria originally was thus encouraged to substantially increase its production of bottled wines. However, when in 1979, Algeria applied for EC aid within the provisions of the 1976 bilateral agreement, to construct two wine-bottling plants, the EC Council of Ministers refused the Algerian request and emphasized the need to reconvert the wine-producing areas to cattle-grazing and raisin production. The reason given was the concern expressed by some member states that surpluses in the Community mitigated against any measure that might help Algeria increase its wine exports to the EC.[19]

Other North African agricultural products, such as citrus fruit, are allowed into EC markets at 80 to 100 per cent tariff reductions, provided that the exporters respect the Community's 'reference prices'. Regarding olive oil, which is of major concern to Tunisia, the exporter is also required to pay an export 'levy' to the Mahgreb country equal to 30 EUA per 100 kg.[20]

The overall impact of the bilateral agreements on the Mahgreb countries (excluding inflationary pressures and changing currency values) has been a reorientation of their exports to different EC member countries. Algeria and Tunisia have been successfully shifting their export patterns away from France toward Germany (in the case of Algeria) and Italy (in the case of Tunisia). Statistics indicate that Germany and Italy are becoming the most important markets for both Mahgreb and Mashreq products.[21]

Despite the EC quotas on textiles and clothing, the Mashreq countries have fared better than their sister states to the West in their trade with EC countries. The most spectacular change in the trade patterns of the Mashreq countries is indicated in the accelerating rate of Egyptian and Syrian exports to EC countries. In an index of the increase in the value of EC imports from the Mahgreb and Mashreq countries in the period 1972–9 (with 1972 = 100), Egypt increased the value of its exports to the EC to 1,250; Syria, correspondingly, raised the value of its exports to 967. (See Table 5.2.)

Such a dramatic increase in trade could be described as a process of 'trade diversion'. The two countries may have been encouraged by their co-operative agreements with the EC,

Table 5.3. Index of the Increase in the Value of European Community
Exports to Arab Mahgreb and Mashreq Countries,
1972-1979 (1972 = 100)

Country	1972	1973	1974	1975	1976	1977	1978	1979
Algeria	100	144	232	328	290	390	436	492
Morocco	100	149	219	311	353	421	410	553
Tunisia	100	138	213	287	304	363	463	549
Mahgreb								
average	100	143.6	221.3	308.6	315.6	367.6	436.3	531.3
Egypt	100	156	311	534	540	614	743	1,019
Jordan	100	131	215	349	590	551	644	946
Lebanon	100	132	206	170	36	151	170	248
Syria	100	154	332	421	674	571	594	846
Mashreq								
average	100	143.3	266	368.5	460	471	537	769.3

Source: International Monetary Fund, *Direction of Trade Statistics Annual*
(Washington DC, IMF, issues 1973-80).

among other factors, to direct their external trade away from
the Soviet Union and Eastern European countries and toward
EC countries.[22] Thus, the Community is becoming a major
trading partner with the Mashreq countries, just as it is today
with the Arab League states as a group. (See also Table 5.3.)

The Enlarged EC and the Mediterranean Policy

The history of the EC's association with the Mediterranean
countries reflects the changes in membership of the former.
In the original EC (composed of six countries) France, as a
Mediterranean country, was the original advocate of associative
diplomacy. Later, Italy became disgruntled over economic
losses and lost opportunities for its farmers as a result of competition from the south and from Spain. Northward expansion
of the Community in 1973 has, however, brought with it the
consolidation of the association system into bilateral and multilateral networks.

It is likely that the entry of Greece into the EC in January
1981 and the anticipated Spanish and Portuguese membership
in 1985 will result in a revision of the essence and structure
of EC Mediterranean policy. The two new members are strong
competitors with the Mahgreb countries. They provide the EC

with the same agricultural products. Tunisia competes directly with Greece and Spain for the Community's market for olive oil. Tunisia currently produces 40 per cent of the Community's olive oil, while Greece and Spain provide 28 per cent and 18 per cent respectively. Spain and Morocco also compete for the Community's citrus market, the former providing 47.1 per cent of its supply and the latter 11.6 per cent.[23]

Agricultural competition between the Mahgreb countries and the new EC members is likely to increase with the inclusion of Portugal, when the full integration of markets in the twelve EC countries takes effect. However, in the opinion of one Community observer, Robert Taylor, the full effect will not be felt for another ten years.[24] The question remains: will the interim period, therefore, bring about the predicted Mediterranean-wide free-trade area? Taylor answers negatively, pointing out that: 'the benefits from privileged access . . . under various preferential agreements have progressively eroded over the past ten years'.[25] In the opinion of this author, a Mediterranean free-trade area is evolving structurally; however, aggregate trade is not necessarily expanding as a result of these structures and institutions.

Spanish, Greek, and Portuguese competition with the Arab Mashreq and Mahgreb countries would not be limited to agricultural products, but would include other industrial products such as textiles, clothing, and shoes. The attempt by Tunisia and Morocco to enlist the support of Arab oil-producing states in the question of textile quotas, within the framework of the Euro–Arab Dialogue, was shrugged off by the EC. Future relief from these export limitations within a larger dialogue would therefore appear most unlikely.[26]

While the proposed southern expansion of the EC may adversely affect the economies of the Mahgreb states, such an expansion would perhaps even change the Community's image abroad, from one of a Northern European power to that of a Mediterranean power. The political ramifications of such a change in image would, perhaps, involve the EC further in Mediterranean political problems. Pressure on the Community to act as a peacemaker in the region would therefore increase, but lack of military capability would rob the Community of effective participation and peace-keeping in any proposed settlement.

Regarding the Arab–Israeli conflict, the three new EC members have traditionally had strong political ties with the Arab world. Spain and Greece do not maintain diplomatic relations with Israel. Unlike other EC member states, who usually abstain from voting on UN resolutions pertinent to the Palestinian question, Spain usually fully backs and in some instances introduces pro-Arab resolutions in the UN General Assembly.[27] However, north European political influence on the new southern members cannot be ruled out. For example, in 1981 it was rumoured in the Arab press that Greece was considering giving in to pressure from other EC members and extending full diplomatic recognition to Israel, something it had not done for the thirty-three years of Israel's existence.[28]

The Bilateral Agreements as a Form of Associative Diplomacy

Associative Diplomacy, which was described earlier as a form of regional dependence, finds its fullest expression in the EC's bilateral agreements with the Arab Mahgreb and Mashreq countries. The agreements were based on the necessity to regulate Community imports in terms of needs. As these needs began to decline over the years through the acquisition of new members and associates, or expanded internal production through various market support mechanisms, the previous dependence on agricultural products from the south also declined and the economic value of these agreements to the EC began to lessen, producing various protection mechanisms or reference prices, levies, and so forth.

The importance to the EC of these association agreements goes beyond immediate economic needs to include other political and strategic considerations. The Community view is that because the Mahgreb countries occupy an important position as the southern gateway to Europe they should be insulated from potential rival powers such as the Soviet Union or China. The French military expedition into Chad in 1979 provides a classic illustration of such considerations.

These political and strategic considerations, as well as a liberalized world-view in the EC Commission, have resulted in continued economic and financial co-operation between the two regions, sometimes in lieu of market access. The attempt by Morocco in 1979 to increase the so-called 'self-limitation'

quotas on canned sardines and tomato concentrate was re-
buffed by the EC Council of Ministers, but instead the Council
offered Morocco an accelerated implementation of aid allocations.[29] EC aid allocations remain, therefore, important for
maintaining the regional dependence of the Mahgreb countries
on EC markets.

European associative diplomacy seems to legitimatize and
expand the scope of the Community's bilateral agreements in
the Arab Mashreq countries as well. Upon the unsuccessful
attempt in 1974 at evoking a multilateral mini-dialogue with
the Organization of Arab Petroleum Exporting Countries
(OAPEC) and the EC, which eventually resulted in merely
a few seminars, the EC extended feelers to several countries in
the Arabian Peninsula. In the spring of 1980, North Yemen,
Bahrain, Oman, Iraq, and Saudi Arabia were contacted. However, only Bahrain, Oman, and North Yemen were very optimistic about the idea of bilateral agreements. In ensuing
diplomatic discussions, Kuwait and Qatar favoured a pan-Gulf
European forum, and Iraq and Saudi Arabia were cool toward
such an approach and favoured a larger pan-Arab/European
dialogue. Only the United Arab Emirates, among the major oil
producers, were responsive to the idea of bilateral co-operation
agreements. The EC emphasized the need to enter into negotiations with the Arab Gulf states in order to avoid future competition from nascent Arab chemical and refined petroleum
industries. The outbreak of hostilities between Iraq and Iran
brought a halt to such plans, since the EC wished to avoid
appearing to support either of the conflicting Gulf states.[30]

The resource-poor states in the Arabian Peninsula, such as
Bahrain and North Yemen, are likely to favour such bilateral
agreements, since they would provide these countries with
some sort of aid. For Bahrain, such co-operative agreements
would also enhance the technical capabilities of that state in
its position as banker of the Gulf area.

For other Arab states, such as Saudi Arabia, bilateral agreements with the EC would hinder long-range goals for the
establishment of their own chemical and fertilizer industries,
particularly in terms of marketing. Saudi Arabia already enjoys
a privileged access to Community markets through the EC
Generalized Scheme of Preferences (GSP). The EC is also the
largest exporter to the Saudi market and benefits from the

kingdom's lowest tariff rates, which average about 3 per cent. If Saudi Arabia committed itself to quotas based on current low-level production it would effectively mortgage its future growth potential in the fertilizer and chemical markets.

Associative diplomacy, as expressed in bilateral trade agreements and export quotas resulting therefrom, remains a mechanism for controlling the future economic and agricultural growth of the Arab Mashreq and Mahgreb states, as well as a means of furthering the Arab political linkage to Europe.

Notes

1. See Article 51 of the Treaty of Rome, in A. J. Peaslee, *International Governmental Organizations' Constitutional Documents*, Part I, Vol. 1 (The Hague, Netherlands, 1974), p. 495.
2. For a systematic differentiation between different association agreements, see J. D. Matthews, *Association System of the European Community* (New York, Praeger, 1977), Chapter 2.
3. R. Ramazani, *The Middle East and the European Common Market* (Charlottesville, University of Virginia Press, 1964), p. 88.
4. W. J. Feld, *The European Community in World Affairs: Economic Power and Political Influence* (Port Washington, New York, Alfred Publishing Co., 1976), p. 148.
5. Ibid., p. 143.
6. European Community Executive Commission, 'Relations with the Mediterranean Countries' (a communication to the EC Council on overall relations between the Community and the Mediterranean countries), *Bulletin of the European Communities*, 10/1 (1977), p. 119.
7. Ibid., p. 120.
8. *Bulletin of the European Communities*, 10/1 (1977), p. 18.
9. For a comparative review of the importance of the Arab world to EC exports over the period 1972-79, see Commission of the European Communities, 'The Development of Trade Between the European Community and the Arab League Countries', *Europe Information Development* (X/278/80-EN, Brussels, September 1980), Table 19b.
10. In a public opinion poll taken by the EC Commission in 1975, 29 per cent of the respondents found it important for the Community to 'pursue a common policy on aid to underdeveloped countries outside Europe'. Seventeen per cent felt it not at all important, and another 17 per cent felt it to be very important; 26 per cent found it of little importance and 11 per cent did not know. Fifty-one per cent of all respondents favoured Community action over national action in this regard. See *Euro-Barometer*, 3/(June–July 1975), Tables 3 and 3a.

11. According to an élite opinion poll conducted by Werner Feld in 1965 and again in 1970, 97 per cent of all respondents saw the 'association agreements as useful instruments of policy', especially in the Mediterranean region. See Feld, op. cit., p. 150.
12. See such an assertion in E. Wallerstein, 'Twenty-Five Years of European Community External Relations', *European Documentation* (journal of the European Community, Brussels) (April 1979), p. 18.
13. For further information see Commission of the European Communities, Spokesman Group and Directorate-General for Information, 'EEC-Morocco Cooperation Agreement', *Europe Information Development* (Brussels, February 1980).
14. Ibid.
15. See, for example, the European Community Executive Commission's information memorandum on the co-operation agreements between the EC and Egypt, Jordan, and Syria (Brussels, EC Executive Commission, December 1976), p. 2.
16. For a further discussion of this point see Feld, op. cit., p. 104.
17. European Communities, European Parliament, *Working Documents 1977-78* (Documents 467-77, 11 January 1978), p. 34.
18. See Article 20 in Commission of the European Communities, Spokesman Group and Directorate-General for Information, *Europe Information Development* (X/123/80, Brussels, June 1980).
19. *Europe Political Day*, 2758 (29 September 1979), p. 9.
20. See Commission of the European Communities, Spokesman Group and Directorate-General for Information, 'EEC-Tunisia Cooperation Agreement', *Europe Information Development* and further revisions in *Europe Political Day*, 2973 (September 1980), p. 1.
21. See a report written by Robert Taylor for the EC Executive Commission, 'Implications for the Southern Mediterranean Countries of the Second Enlargement of the European Community', *Europe Information Development* (X/225/80-EN, Brussels, June 1980), see particularly Table XVI.
22. In the interim, Syria's exports to the USSR also increased but at a very much slower rate. Egypt's exports to the USSR have, however, decreased during the same period, particularly in 1978 and 1979. See International Monetary Fund, *Direction of Trade Statistics Annual* (Washington DC, IMF, 1980), pp. 356-444.
23. Taylor, op. cit., Table VIII.
24. Ibid., p. 22.
25. Ibid.
26. For example, at the Brussels conference, Tunisia attempted to focus the attention of the commerce committee of the Euro-Arab Dialogue exclusively on the subject of textiles. See Euro-Arab Dialogue, General Committee, 'Final Communiqué', Brussels, 26-28 October 1977 (Brussels, Commission of the European Communities), p. 14.

27. See, for example, US Resolution A/35/L38, 16 December 1980, which was authored by Spain and was intended as an amendment to UN Resolution 242 of 1967. The former was voted against by a majority of EC countries, with the exception of France and Greece who abstained. Incidentally, this was the first time Greece had abstained on a Palestinian-related resolution.
28. *Al-Bilad* (16 April 1981), p. 3.
29. See EC–Morocco Co-operation Council, Joint Press Release (CEE–MA 2708/79, Brussels, 15 June 1979).
30. Based on personal interviews by the author conducted at the offices of the EC Commission in Brussels on 25 November 1980.

6 THE EUROPEAN COMMUNITY AND ARAB FUNDS CO-FINANCING OF DEVELOPMENT PROJECTS IN AFRICA

To appreciate fully the nuances of the European Community (EC) approach toward the Arab World, one needs to examine the slowly evolving pattern of Euro–Arab co-operation in the financing of development projects in Africa, particularly those projects implemented in countries south of the Sahara. The EC has been involved since 1975 in a major development programme amounting to some 3,457 million European Units of Account (EUA) and benefiting more than fifty-two countries in Africa, the Caribbean, and the Pacific (the ACP countries). The Lomé group of associated countries, as it became known, renegotiated the earlier agreement with the Community in 1979 and succeeded in obtaining an increase in EC aid allocation of 5,692 EUA over the subsequent five-year period. Lomé I and Lomé II formed a massive development enterprise involving a total commitment of over 9 billion EUA over a ten-year period.[1]

Similarly, the national funds of various Arab countries have been used individually and collectively to finance several development projects in Africa. Disbursement of this aid to countries south of the Sahara has largely tended to be of a bilateral nature, channelled via Arab national funds, and has increased from approximately $400 million in 1975 to $543.8 billion in 1979.[2]

Arab aid is distributed by several public and private institutions most of which, except for the Kuwaiti fund, were established after 1973.[3] The growth of capital surpluses in the Gulf area necessitated the build-up of new financial institutions through which surplus funds could be channelled toward other Arab and underdeveloped countries. Most of these new institutions followed the same structure as the existing major international development bodies such as the World Bank and the International Bank for Reconstruction and Development

(IBRD). Many of these existing institutions helped to provide technical assistance for the emerging Arab funds.

Unlike the Kuwaiti Fund for Arab Economic Development, which was established in 1961, the new Arab funds did not have the time or the technical capability to develop their own identification, appraisal, and implementation systems. Therefore, they had to rely on other international institutions for the purposes of identifying specific aid ventures. Among the international aid-giving banks which had a list of ready-for-financing projects were the World Bank and the European Development Fund (EDF).[4]

The Concept of Co-financing

The practice of co-financing among international aid-giving public agencies began in the 1950s, when some newly established Swedish and Norwegian aid agencies sought to enter the aid field without the necessary experience in project management in Third World countries. The first seventeen projects co-financed between Sweden and the World Bank were carried out in Bangladesh and India.[5] The Kuwaiti Fund for Arab Economic Development also participated with the World Bank in co-financing projects in North Yemen and in Jordan.[6]

The 'leading' or managing institution need not be the major contributor of funds but may reap 35 per cent of the total cost in service fees. These fees can provide a bank with good earnings.[7] Co-financing benefits a bank in other ways. It liberates the bank's own funds for use in other sectors or projects, hence expanding the bank's activities. For instance, the World Bank's group (the IBRD and the IDA) matched external public funds to finance 80 per cent of its own aid commitment in 1979. For the bank contribution of $4.1 billion in loans to underdeveloped countries, another $3.2 billion were matched from external public sources and $550 million were mobilized from the private sector.[8]

In a similar fashion, the EC and its development agencies (the EDF and the European Investment Bank (EIB)) have increasingly relied on co-financing schemes to support their development programmes in Africa. Such co-financing was engaged in first with the World Bank group and later with the

Arab national funds. Co-financing, thus far, has supported 67 per cent of the EC's disbursed commitments under Lomé I (1975–80), and a good part of these funds have been provided from the recipient countries themselves.[9]

Co-financing development projects in underdeveloped areas with European technology and Arab money was given an intellectual *vis a tergo* by the creation in 1979 of the Group of Paris, a private group led by the French intellectual Jean-Jacques Servan Schreiber. The group works for an alliance between the Arab world, Europe, Japan, and Africa to finance the required transfer of technology to eliminate backwardness and poverty. The group is structured on the lines of the Tri-lateral Commission,[10] which brings together policy makers in Europe, Japan, and the United States in formal discussion, and has been instrumental in the creation of a number of Euro–Arab colloquies on the co-financing of development, one of which was held in Kuwait in April 1981.

The EC's policy of co-financing seeks to structurally associate the Arab oil-producing countries, the EC, and the oil-deficient, underdeveloped countries through European development channels. Such a flow not only increases the size of available funds, but also brings the two sides of the triangle closer to the Community through dependence on the Community's aid mechanism.

The rationale behind this arrangement is that it provides additional allocations of aid to developing countries, brings efficiency and harmony to the planning and execution of projects, and minimizes the enormous cost of financing major schemes such as dams, railroads, or irrigation projects. The EC's co-financing activities in co-operation with Arab national funds is, in addition, an attempt to recycle Arab petro-dollars. Such a scheme would 'intensify consumption of the capital available for development'.[11]

EC co-financing with the Arab funds dates back to 1975 when the EDF joined five other development banks, including the Arab Bank for Economic Development in Africa (ABEDA) in financing the Douala port in Cameroon. Other co-financed projects quickly followed in the same year, including a road project in Mauritania that brought three other Arab funds into joint financing efforts with the Community.[12] In the ensuing six years the number of co-financed projects has reached twenty-one, eighteen of which were carried out in Africa, south of the Sahara.[13]

Community co-financing with the Arab funds would have been a routine form of financial collaboration, except that it has lately been elevated to the realm of high politics. At the European summit meeting in Venice in June 1980 the participants made a point of stressing the need to recycle Arab oil money to 'attenuate the negative effects of these (balance of payments) imbalances' on underdeveloped countries.[14]

The Western economic summit meeting in Venice later that same month called even more explicitly for increased efforts in co-financing:

The democratic industrialized countries cannot alone carry the responsibility of aid and other different contributions to developing countries; it must be equitably shared by the oil-exporting countries and the industrialized Communist countries. The Personal Representatives are instructed to view aid policies and procedures and other contributions to developing countries and to report back their conclusions to the next Summit.[15]

By November 1980 such a review had already been undertaken by the EC Commission. The Commission's review also stressed that co-financing should be 'voluntary' and regional in perspective, and that it should be encouraged by all oil-producing countries, be they in the Arab world or in the Caribbean (Venezuela, Mexico, Trinidad, and Tobago), and should 'be aimed at assisting non-oil-producing LDCs in that region'.[16]

The EC is willing to lend management and technical assistance in the implementation of co-financed projects through the Commission's delegations in various ACP and Mediterranean capitals. As to procurement policies, the Community is willing to relax its condition of tendering to non-EC suppliers 'provided of course that the other cofinancing parties make the same concessions and agree to European firms being eligible'.[17]

The Response of Arab Funds to Co-financing

Unlike the national funds, Arab multilateral funds, such as the ABEDA and the OPEC funds, have expressed more enthusiasm for joint financing with EC funds. The national funds, such as the Kuwaiti fund and the Saudi fund, have more staff and, in the case of the Kuwaiti fund, more experienced in independent evaluation of development projects.

The Kuwaiti fund has a technical assistance programme of its own. Its technical teams helped North Yemen to set up the Yemeni Industrial Bank in 1976. The Kuwaiti fund was also instrumental in the establishment of several major Arab aid funds such as the ABEDA and the Inter-Arab Investment Guarantee Corporation.[18]

The Arab national funds, therefore, have been more interested in parallel financing than in joint financing, since they act independently from other international aid donors while tapping the others' project identification capabilities. The administrators of the funds have been wary of the long-term commitments that might be required in more formal arrangements. They advance the notion that their organizations are 'development institutions', not merely providers of funds. They are of the opinion that 'grandoise schemes' might, in effect, deprive the funds of their financial autonomy, and that 'institutionalized frameworks' might pit them against their own allies in the Third World.[19]

As multilateral institutions, both the ABEDA and the OPEC fund benefit from opportunities for 'gap-financing' in multilateral schemes. In their cases, the emphasis on co-financing is explicitly stated in their own characters. Co-financing, therefore, is viewed as a speedy method of aid disbursement and, in practice, the majority of OPEC fund financing has been channelled through joint financing schemes.[20]

The EC aid policy is a programmatic one that is determined on a regional basis over a given number of years. For instance, the Community committed itself to providing southern Mediterranean Arab countries with a package of 639 million EUA over a four-year period. On the other hand, the Arab countries (except for the multilateral institutions), have maintained an aid policy on a year-by-year basis and toward specific recipients, such as the Arab 'confrontational states' or Africa, as in the $1.45 billion committed at the Cairo Arab–African summit conference of 1977.[21]

The Arab funds have generally steered away from grand aid schemes. The exceptions have been Arab contributions to the International Fund for Agricultural Development and to other UN programmes. However, in 1980, Iraq suggested a plan in which the Arab oil producers would offer rebates to under-developed countries based on the increased cost of oil to them, while the industrialized countries would match these with such rebates as were necessary due to their own inflation-inducing increases in the cost of manufactured goods. The combined input would then be deposited in a co-finance fund for balance of payments supports to LDCs. If such a plan were implemented, it would act as an aid buffer-reserve that would help alleviate the chronic developmental needs of the LDCs.[22]

The Modalities of Co-financing

The tapping of Arab funds by the EC has been largely directed toward alleviating the budgetary burdens of the Community with regard to its commitments to the ACP countries. As noted earlier, Lomé I obligated the Community to contribute 3,456 million EUA over the five-year period 1975–80. A massive commitment of this size called for the enlistment of financial support from other international lenders and donors through the mechanism of co-financing, or trilateral co-operation.

Administrators of the Arab national funds usually extend loans to underdeveloped countries through either a balance of payments assistance or through direct project lending. It is the latter which directly activates the co-financing links with other international institutions. The EDF, just like the World Bank, periodically publishes a list of suggested projects, some of which have been merely identified and others which have been studied and perhaps even evaluated in terms of estimated cost. The 'project profile' list is usually published in English and in French, and contains information pertaining to the country, the title of the projects, the objectives, details, costs, financing, and project status. Such a list is circulated among potential financiers and is periodically updated.[23] An Arab or inter-national bank may then express a tentative interest or a full commitment to subscribe to the financing effort of a given project. Such interest may be limited to a single year of financ-ing or to a single part of the project, since some projects are ongoing enterprises. Budgetary constraints may limit the participation of the fund in the first year, but more allocations may be forthcoming in future years.

Finally, co-operation in co-financing with the Arab funds

Table 6.1. Projects Co-financed by the European Community and Arab Funds (1975–1981) (in $US millions*)

Country	Project	Cost	Country or self-financing	EC				Arab funds	IBRD	Others
				Commission	EIB	States	Total			
1 Cameroon	Douala port	125.8	17.8	5.6	–	16.4	22	11.2	28.1	46.8
2 Cameroon	Songloulo barrage	257.7	127.8	–	17.9	47.2	65.1	64.8	–	–
3 Comores	Telecommunications	4.6	–	3.1	–	–	3.1	1.6	–	–
4 Congo	CFCO	343.5	40	49.3	–	39.9	89.2	102	60.5	51.7
5 Ghana	Kpong dam	283.4	77.9	11.9	13.3	–	25.3	87.2	46.8	46.1
6 Guinea	Plastic factory	17.3	3.3	7.7	–	–	7.7	6.2	–	–
7 Upper Volta	Poura goldmine	61.3	1.7	10.8	15.3	17	43.1	3.6	–	11.9
8 Lesotho	Massero airport	45.2	2.9	3.9	–	–	3.9	23.5	–	14.8
9 Liberia	Central part of Bushrod road	31.9	1.7	–	6.5	–	6.5	15.7	7.9	–
10 Mali	Silingue barrage	171.9	–	30.9	–	42.9	73.9	73.1	–	24.8
11 Mo	Hydroelectric scheme	50.9	10.6	–	9.9	13.6	23.5	16.8	–	–
12 Mauritania	Guels iron	463.8	148.5	–	33.2	48.3	81.5	164.2	57.9	11.6
13 Mauritania	Gorgol	93.2	9.6	12.5	–	12.5	25	30.6	11.6	16.5
14 Rwanda	Mukungwa	39.6	3.6	26.6	–	–	26.6	9.4	–	–
15 Somalia	Goluen-Gelib road	70.9	2	36.8	–	–	36.8	22.1	–	–

16 Somalia	Bardheera dam	465.4	26.6	58.5	–	114.4	172.9	23.9	–	242
17 Sudan	Babanoussa railway	167.1	81.5	11.9	–	–	11.9	50.9	22.7	–
18 Togo/Ghana/Ivory Coast	Cimo cement complex	331.6	71.7	23.9	34.4	48.3	106.6	11.7	70	71.5
19 Mauritania/Senegal/Mali	OMVS	706.1	–	19.9	–	165.3	185.2	200.4	–	320.5
20 Cameroon/Chad	Gidjiba/Moundou road	82.5	–	13.3	–	–	13.3	16.9	33.2	19
21 Zaïre/Zambia/Angola	Lobito road	34.7	–	10.6	34.6	6.6	17.3	14	–	3.5
22 Morocco	Jorf Lasfer port	292.5	202.1	18.6	–	–	53.2	37.2	–	–
23 Egypt	Development of Suez Canal	1,252.6	691.5	–	33.2	10.6	43.8	148.9	106.4	261.9
24 Syria	Aleppo/Tal Kojak road	170.2	114.1	4.7	22.6	–	27.3	10.6	18.2	–
25 Indonesia	The Salawesi trans-migration	86.2	35.9	6.4	–	–	6.4	10.6	–	33.2
TOTAL		5,640.2	1,670.9	367.3	221.1	582.9	1,171.4	1,157.3	463.5	1,176.9
Percentage		100	29.6	6.5	3.9	10.4	20.8	20.5	8.2	20.9

*Figures are converted from EUA (6 November 1980, 1 EUA = $1.32977), and rounded to the nearest tenth of $US millions.
Source: Commission of the European Communities, Directorate-General for Development, *Community Involvement in Co-financing* (Brussels, 11 November 1980), Annex 11.

seems to be largely functional in nature. In an interview with this author, a member of the EC Commission commented: 'Unlike the Euro–Arab Dialogue we [Arab and European fund administrators] have been cooperating for five years with no political advocation.'[24] It may have escaped the attention of this Commission member that by associating the Arab funds with the Community's development efforts, political policies were being conducted through financial means.

Patterns of Euro–Arab Co-financing

Co-financing schemes between the Community and the various Arab national funds have largely tended to concentrate on infrastructure projects. Out of the twenty-five joint development projects, seventeen have been infrastructure projects (roads, dams, railways, etc.).[25] The high cost of these projects and the aversion on the part of Arab fund administrators to these types of projects (which is perhaps based on the high visibility of the projects) have made them good candidates for co-financing.

The majority of the co-financed projects are in Africa. Out of a total of twenty-five projects in 1975–81, twenty-one were in Africa, three in the Mashreq countries, and one in Indonesia. (See Table 6.1.) The largest single contribution of Arab funds to co-financed projects has been the extension of a 150 million EUA ($200 million) loan to finance a bridge-barrage project benefiting Mauritania, Senegal, and Mali.

The Arab funds usually subscribe from 8 to 36 per cent of the cost of an individual project. Arab participation in completed, co-financed Lomé I projects has, however, reached 36 per cent.[26] Total Arab contributions of the costs of all co-financed projects between 1975–81 were, however, smaller, amounting to only 20.5 per cent (see Table 6.1).

Combined EC contributions to projects co-financed with the Arab funds in Lomé I reached 31.3 per cent. However, total EC contributions to all co-financed projects are lower, totalling 20.8 per cent.[27] These figures suggest that 45 per cent of the costs of all co-financed EC commitments were borne by the Arab funds.

Further comparison of the figures with other OECD–DAC estimates of Arab contributions and loans to Africa over the period 1975–80 ($2.1 billion) suggests that one-third of all Arab aid to Africa went directly through European channels. These facts may have encouraged the EDF to pursue with vigour its financial collaboration with the Arab funds, which passed the 20 per cent mark in 1980. (See Figure 6.1.)

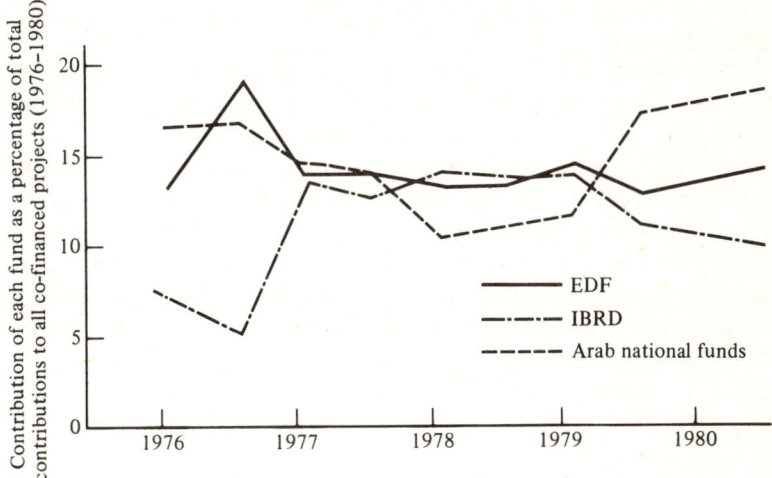

Fig. 6.1. Evolution of EDF Co-financing with the Arab National Funds and the IBRD Funds.

Co-financing as a Form of Associative Diplomacy

The co-financing triad (EC–Arab–African) approach is yet another attempt to recycle surpluses and introduce a new order of management of aid allocation to underdeveloped countries and regions. It ensures the continued adherence of the two regions to the EC banking establishments, namely the EDF and the EIB, and alleviates the burden of aid contributions on the Community's own resources.

The regionalization of these loans is a remarkable innovation. It is based on the contention that the rich members of an international region ought to alleviate, through a third-party catalyst, the poverty of their neighbours and brethren. Such a contention may appear to be an egalitarian and commendable proposition. But the question remains as to why these funds must go through European or extra-regional channels.

European defendants of such a policy have alluded to its efficiency and lack of duplication of administrative effort.[28] These reasons, while judicious, must, however, be regarded as secondary to other implicit mercantilist and political motives. Co-financing schemes assure European suppliers and contractors of a steady flow of construction projects in Africa and cultivate goodwill toward the EC in Africa, particularly if the projects are highly visible.

The contention that co-financing schemes act as a 'catalyst' for the mobilization of other funds for development purposes cannot be proven. Over the past five years, Arab aid commitment has been a function of the total oil earnings of these countries; that is, it declined in 1977 and 1978, and experienced some growth in 1979. While the period of examination is rather short, the co-financing period may have proved more important in redirecting the relative flow of Arab assistance commitments away from major Arab recipients, and increasingly toward Africa.[29]

Notes

1. For a brief review of the Community's commitment of Lomé I and Lomé II see 'Community Aid to the Third World: The Lomé Connection', *European File* (March and June 1981).
2. Such sums also include aid allocations by other OPEC members: Iran, Nigeria, and Venezuela. It does not, however, include multilateral Arab aid allocations totalling $158 million in 1975 and $271 million in 1979. See OECD-DAC, *Development Cooperation, 1979 Review*, Tables G.7 and X.2, and OECD-DAC, *Development Cooperation, 1980 Review*, Tables G.7 and VII-5 (Paris, OECD-DAC, November 1980 and November 1981).
3. The nine Arab national funds co-operating with the Community aid institutions in co-financing are: the Abu Dhabi Fund for Arab Economic Development (AFAED), the Saudi Development Fund (SDF), the Arab Bank for Economic Development in Africa (ABEDA), the Arab Fund for Economic and Social Development (AFESD), the Islamic Development Bank (ISB), the Iraqi Fund, the Kuwaiti Fund for Arab Economic Development (KFAED), the OPEC fund, and the Qatari fund.
4. See the World Bank Group, *Policies and Operations* (Washington DC, World Bank Group, September 1974), p. 59.
5. Ibid., p. 61.
6. Ibid.

7. Ibid., p. 8. See also World Bank, *Cofinancing Review of the World Bank Activities* (Washington DC, World Bank, December 1976).
8. OECD–DAC, *Development Cooperation, 1980 Review*, as cited in Note 2, p. 166.
9. See Commission of the European Communities, Directorate–General for Development, *Community Involvement in Cofinancing* (Brussels, 11 November 1980), Annex 5.
10. See J.-J. Servan-Schreiber, *The World Challenge* (New York, Simon and Schuster, 1981). See also his article 'The Day America Wakes Up: A Challenge from the New Pioneers', *Los Angeles Times* (12 July 1981), Part IV, pp. 1–3.
11. Commission of the European Communities, Directorate-General for Development, op. cit., p. 4.
12. The funds are the Kuwaiti fund, the Abu Dhabi fund, and the Arab Fund for Economic and Social Development. See T. Scharf, *Trilateral Cooperation*, Vol. 1 *Arab Development Funds and Banks: Approaches to Trilateral Cooperation* (Paris, OECD Development Centre Studies, 1978), Table 4, G-III.
13. Commission of the European Communities, Directorate-General for Development, op. cit., Annexes 6 and 7.
14. 'Summary of the Presidency of the Proceedings of the European Council', *Bulletin of the European Communities*, 13/6 (1980), p. 9.
15. See Article 26 of the Western Economic Summit Declaration in *Bulletin of the European Communities*, 13/6 (1980), p. 7.
16. Commission of the European Communities, Directorate-General for Development, op. cit., p. 1.
17. Ibid., p. 5.
18. S. Demir, *Arab Development Funds in the Middle East* (New York, Pergamon Press for UNITAR, 1979), p. 8 and Table 1.2.
19. See the paper written by Z. A. Nasr, an economic advisor to the Kuwaiti fund, in Scharf, op. cit., Vol. II, and the proceedings and background papers of a conference organized by the OECD and held on 26-7 January 1978 in Paris, in Scharf, op. cit., Vol. I, pp. 71–80. See also A. al-Hamad, director-general of the KFAED, *Some Aspects of the Kuwait Fund's Approach to International Development Assistance* (Kuwait, Kuwaiti Fund for Arab Development, 1977).
20. I. Shihata, director-general of the OPEC fund, 'Cofinancing and the OPEC Special Fund', *Development Digest*, 4 (October 1979), 55–62.
21. See 'Arab Aid to Africa: The Arab Bank for Economic Development in Africa and the Arab Fund for Technical Assistance to African and Arab Countries', *OAPEC Bulletin*, 4/7 (July 1978), pp. 22–6. See also V. LeVine and T. W. Luke, *The Arab-African Connection: Political and Economic Realities* (Boulder, Colo., Westview Press, 1979), p. 20.
22. For further details, see an interview with Dr A. A. al-Anbari, director

of the Iraqi Fund for External Development, in 'Iraqi Aid Totals 3.2% of GNP', *OAPEC Bulletin*, 7/1 (January 1981), p. 16.

23. See, for example, the project profile of the realignment of the Douala-Yaoundé railway in the report of the Commission of the European Communities, *Summary of Projects for Possible Cofinancing in the Context of Lomé II* (Brussels, September 1980).
24. Personal interview at EC Commission offices, Brussels, 24 November 1980.
25. Based on lists of projects provided to the author by the EC Commission.
26. See, 'Community-Arab Funds Cofinancing meeting of June 18, 1980' (Brussels, 18 June 1980).
27. Ibid.
28. See Scharf, op. cit., Vol. 1.
29. See OECD-DAC, *Development Cooperation, 1980 Review*, as cited in Note 2, p. 168 and Table G.5.

PART III

THE ENVIRONMENT OF ASSOCIATIVE DIPLOMACY

7 WESTERN EUROPE AND THE
   PALESTINIAN QUESTION

Through three Arab–Israeli wars (1948, 1956, and 1967) Europe played a major military and political role in shaping the future of the modern Arab world. This role was not always negative. The Europeans introduced modern education and health facilities, but for the most part the European political system controlled and directed the evolution of the Arab political system. The year of 1973 was a watershed: for the first time in this century, developments within the Arab political system 'spilled over' into Europe.

Europe had no choice. It was linked economically and politically to the Arab world and, as history would dictate, had become part of the moral and political nexus of the Palestinian question. If the Europe of the 1880s wrestled with the Jewish question, then the Europe of the 1970s and 1980s is wrestling with the Palestinian question. This political and moral dictate conditions (for the Europeans) and governs (for the Arabs) any form of associative diplomatic policies adopted by their respective regional entities. This interlock between the political milieu and geo-economic politics is an undeniable fact that has continuously haunted any regional policy and has determined its success or failure.

This chapter will discuss the importance of the Palestinian question to the success of European associative diplomacy. We will see that the depicted change of political policies in Western Europe over the last seven years has been primarily collectively voiced through the European Political Co-operation System (EPCS) and influenced by Arab political demands voiced in the Euro–Arab Dialogue.

The Palestinian Problem in the Context of European Associative Diplomacy

Within the milieu of associative diplomacy, the Palestinian question and its resolution, based on equilibrium and justice, is the arch concern of the Arab states. No regional or national programme of economic development is complete without recognition of the security constraint. We have seen many economic and civilian installations ravaged by Israeli military attacks. The preoccupation with security and the seeking of European diplomatic support for a peaceful resolution of the conflict has governed Arab relations with the European Community (EC), particularly in the Euro–Arab Dialogue.

In the Arab view, Western Europe, through the aegis of the Community and the EPCS, can and does exert influence in determining developments in the Arab region. Bilateral EC agreements with Israel have almost wrecked the Euro–Arab Dialogue, but sincere efforts on both sides have kept it on its track. For the Arab states and their league, the life and vitality of European associative diplomacy is dependent upon the diplomatic recognition and support of the Palestine Liberation Organization (PLO) as the sole representative of the Palestinian people.

The Arabs further view Europe as the intellectual mantle of American foreign policy. They point to the traditional role played by the United Kingdom in giving essence and spirit to American foreign policy,[1] and they hope that such an effort will also be exerted on their behalf in Washington. Many Arab states, had it not been for the perceived American support of Israel, would today be close allies of the United States. The intermediary role played by Europe as a bridge to America (in addition to serving as the so-called 'third alternative'), and the central role played by Europe in keeping the Arab world from total alienation from the West, are important factors giving continued impetus to the process of associative diplomacy.

Europe, on the other hand, initially felt that associative diplomacy could stand on its own feet through complementarity of energy and advanced technology. Qualitative and quantitative aid directed through the structures of associative diplomacy was considered sufficient impetus to any meaningful dialogue with the Arabs. Today on the European scene even the most ardent supporter of Israel recognizes the importance of peace for the economic and political security of Europe itself.[2]

Reasons of political and economic security have pushed the Europeans to a diplomatic and political stance that may not be to the liking of Washington. Their reserved support for the Camp David accords and their implied recognition of the PLO have distinguished them from their American allies. The EC, as a trading bloc, will always require secure access to oil and other raw materials. Exhaustion of these resources on the Continent continues to give impetus to the search for new supply sources or to the securing of old ones, whether they be in Africa, the Arab world, or even in Siberia.

European Council Statements on the Palestinian Question

Official European opinion within the EPCS has been voiced since 1973 in the joint communiqués of the presidents and the annual statements made by the foreign ministers of the member states at the United Nations. European views on the Middle East have sprung from a need to reassert a European voice in any political settlement in the Middle East. In the words of former French President, the late Georges Pompidou, at the conclusion of the 1973 Arab–Israeli war:

We are obligated to find that the cease fire and efforts toward opening negotiations were prepared and effected with no participation by Europe in any form whatsover. Because of this and many other reasons . . . it seems to me to be absolutely necessary to provide manifold proof of the solidarity behind the construction of Europe and her capacity to help in settling world problems.[3]

At an emergency meeting of the foreign ministers of the EC member countries on 5–6 November 1973, the EC agreed on a four-point declaration which included the following guiding principles for a peaceful settlement of the Palestinian question:
(1) The inadmissability of the acquisition of territory by force;
(2) The need for Israel to end the territorial occupation which it has maintained since the conflict of 1967;
(3) Respect for the sovereignty, territorial integrity, and independence of every state in the area and their right to live in peace with secure and recognized boundaries;
(4) Recognition that a just and lasting peace must take into account the legitimate rights of the Palestinians.[4]
The four guiding principles encompass the same elements of UN Resolution 242 (of 1967), in addition to an important addition that goes beyond the resolution—namely, the need

to recognize the Palestinians as a people without a homeland, something the UN resolution had evaded. Since 1973, the principles have become the cornerstone of the EC approach to the Palestinian problem.

A month after this declaration, the European Council summit meeting in Copenhagen went further and called for the participation of all the parties to the dispute in a conference at Geneva, and expressed its readiness to guarantee a settlement in the region.[5] Its representatives at the UN General Assembly voted for a resolution inviting the PLO to participate in the proposed Geneva conference in the Middle East. Ironically, Israel and the US voted in favour of this resolution, but all of the Arab countries (with the exception of Syria, who abstained) voted against it.[6] Israel, at a later date, however, insisted on the exclusion of the PLO from the meeting, which was held on 21–2 December 1975, and neither Syria nor the PLO attended the meeting.[7]

Four years after the November 1973 declaration, the London summit meeting of the EC (on 29–30 June 1977) produced an amendment to the earlier declaration and explained 'the legitimate rights of the Palestinian "national identity" ', and identified 'a need for a homeland for the Palestinian people'. The amendment stated:

The Nine have affirmed their belief that a solution to the conflict in the Middle East will be possible only if the legitimate rights of the Palestinian people to give effective expression to its national identity is translated into fact, which would take into account the need for a homeland for the Palestinian people. They consider that the representatives of the parties to the conflict, including the Palestinian people, must participate in the negotiations in an appropriate manner to be worked out in consultation between all the parties concerned.[8]

Such a declaration was received with enthusiasm by the Arab world, and many Arab observers were counting the days before the EC would formally recognize the PLO as the sole representative of the Palestinian people. At the UN, the EC countries went on record for the first time as opposing the establishment of Israeli settlements in the occupied Arab territories. This was a further departure from their earlier pattern of abstaining on UN resolutions dealing with the Palestinian question.[9]

The Camp David agreement, negotiated by the US between

Egypt and Israel in September 1978, brought about an expression of reserved support from the Community. In their communiqué of 19 September 1978, the EC foreign ministers, meeting in Bonn, refrained from fully backing the accord, due to French insistence, and instead issued a carefully worded statement in which they supported the agreement but qualified that support by emphasizing the primacy of a comprehensive rather than separate or partial settlement. In their view, 'the outcome is hoped to be a major step on the path to a just, comprehensive and lasting peace, and that all parties concerned will find it possible to join in the process to contribute to that end'.[10]

At the UN one week later, speaking on behalf of the Community, Hans-Dietrich Genscher, the German Foreign Minister, went out of his way to reassure the Arab world—which had emphatically rejected the Camp David agreement as merely a partial peace—of the imperative of a comprehensive settlement based on recognition of Palestinian rights. The statement, however, reflected the German feeling that the partial nature of the agreement should not preclude the participation of the others, and it acceded to French and Arab demands that any peace agreement should be comprehensive and address the genesis of the problem, namely a Palestinian homeland. Genscher said:

If such a peace settlement is to be achieved, it is imperative that all parties concerned participate in its negotiation and completion. Meanwhile, no obstacle should be placed in the way of this process, which should be kept open, and should, through further development and wider participation, lead to a comprehensive settlement.[11]

The EC foreign ministers, meeting a few months later in Paris (26 March 1979) at a General Assembly of the Western European Union issued another statement in which they belatedly supported the Israeli–Egyptian peace treaty. They nevertheless viewed it as part of a full implementation of UN Resolutions 242 and 338. They also re-emphasized the need for a Palestinian homeland. In an indirect criticism of declared US policy, they endorsed the need for Palestinian participation in the negotiations and once again reasserted the right of the Palestinian people to a homeland, without necessarily the participation of the PLO. 'The international community', in their view, 'could give its backing . . . to representatives of the Palestinian people'.[12]

In two separate clauses, the nine EC foreign ministers, meeting in Paris on 18 June 1979 at a General Assembly of the Western European Union, condemned Israeli violation of UN Resolution 242, which stated the principle of the 'inadmissability of the acquisition of territory by force'.[13] They also emphasized the illegality of Israeli settlements in occupied Arab territories.

The Irish Foreign Minister, Michael O'Kennedy, speaking on behalf of the Community at a UN General Assembly for the Palestinian people in the autumn of 1979, redefined European peace proposals to include 'the right to a homeland, and the right, through its representatives, to play its full part in the negotiation of a comprehensive settlement'. He also declared that 'in the view of the Nine, it is necessary that they be accepted [UN Resolutions 242 of 1967, and 338 of 1978] by all those involved, including the Palestine Liberation Organization'.[14]

On the question of illegal annexation by Israel of East Jerusalem, O'Kennedy differentiated the question of access to the Holy Places from the formal status of the city:

The Nine are fully aware, too, of the importance of the Question of Jerusalem to all parties. They know that an acceptable solution to this problem will be vital to an overall settlement on the basis I have indicated. They consider, in particular, that any agreement on the future status of Jerusalem should guarantee free access by all to the Holy Places; and they do not accept any unilateral moves which claim to change the status of the city.[15]

The European Initiative on the Middle East

Due to major obstacles facing the American-sponsored talks between Egypt and Israel on Palestinian autonomy, which reached a stalemate in the spring of 1980, and as a continuation of the German-sponsored initiative on the Middle East which had begun a year earlier, the EC meeting in Venice on 12–13 June 1980 marked the launching of a major European peace initiative on the Middle East.

In the days preceding the Venice meeting, there was a strong impression in European and Arab political circles that the EC countries were about to officially recognize the PLO. However, there were strong reactions from US President Jimmy Carter and Israeli Prime Minister Menachem Begin. The latter sent his Foreign Minister, Yitzak Shamir, to visit six European capitals on 9–10 June 1980, to line up votes against the German–French initiative at the Venice meeting. Shamir met on 9 June with Belgian Foreign Minister Nothomb and with EC commissioners Haferkamp and Cheysson, as well as with the EC president, Roy Jenkins, and the president-designate Gaston Thorn, to effect a change in the language of the proposed declaration.[16]

American fears of possible European recognition of the PLO were allayed through the dispatch on 12 June of a special EC envoy, Emilio Colombo, to Washington to assure the US government of the 'identity which exists between the United States and Europe on a series of international issues'.[17] Herr Genscher of Germany also went out of his way, through a press conference in Bonn on the eve of the Venice meeting, to assure Israel and the US that 'the Community does not intend proposing a change in the UN Security Council resolution 242',[18] which meant that the EC would not recognize the PLO. Last-minute Arab lobbying efforts in Europe by the Iraqi Foreign Minister on 12 June did not succeed in countering intense Israeli and US pressure.[19]

The Venice declaration not only reiterated the earlier declarations of the EC, but for the first time pointed to the need for 'associating' the PLO with any peaceful settlement in the region. The summit meeting also sent Gaston Thorn, the Luxembourg Foreign Minister and the new president of the EC Council, to tour the area to sound out the views of the Arabs and Israelis on the European peace plan.

The Venice statement included a seven-point European initiative for establishing peace in the region. (See Appendix B for the full text of the initiative.) In summary, the seven points were:

(1) The right to existence and to security of all of the states in the region, including Israel, and justice for all the peoples which implies recognition of the legitimate rights of the Palestinian people.
(2) All of the countries in the area are entitled to live in peace with secure, recognized, and guaranteed borders . . . The Nine declare that they are prepared to participate within the framework of a

comprehensive settlement in a system of concrete and binding international guarantees, including [guarantees] on the ground.

(3) A just solution must finally be found to the Palestinian problem,
which is not simply one of refugees. The Palestinian people, which is
conscious of existing as such, must be placed in a position, by an
appropriate process defined within the framework of the comprehensive peace settlement, to exercise fully its right to self-determination.

(4) The achievement of these objectives requires the involvement and
support of all of the parties concerned in the peace settlement which
the Nine are endeavouring to promote in keeping with the principles
formulated in the declaration referred to above. These principles
apply to all the parties concerned, and thus to the Palestinian people,
and to the PLO, which will have to be associated with the negotiations.

(5) The Nine stress the need for Israel to put an end to the territorial
occupation which it has maintained since the conflict of 1967, as it
has done for part of Sinai. They are deeply convinced that the Israeli
settlements constitute a serious obstacle to the peace process of the
Middle East. The Nine consider that these settlements, as well as
modification in population and property in the occupied territories,
are illegal under international law.

(7) Concerned as they are to put an end to violence, the Nine consider
that only the renunciation of force or threatened use of force by all
the parties can create a climate of confidence in the area and constitute a basic element for a comprehensive settlement of the conflict
in the Middle East.[20]

Registered Arab reaction to the plan varied from total support by the Egyptians, 'as long as it is in the context of the
Camp David agreements', to that of the Jordanian Prime Minister who called the proposal a 'positive step in the right direction
but in itself inadequate'.[21]

Within the PLO, the Democratic Front for the Liberation of
Palestine labelled the European declaration 'a small step in the
right direction'; PLO chairman, Yasser Arafat, recognized 'some
contradictions and ambiguities' in the European statement;
Farouq Kadoumi, the PLO foreign minister, expressed some
optimism about the European declaration, claiming that it 'contains important and positive elements'.[22]

Israeli Prime Minsiter Begin emphatically rejected PLO
participation in the peace process, and labelled the European
plan a 'Munich-type abdication . . . in the face of blackmail
from all elements who want to undermine the Camp David
agreements and foil the chances of peace in the Middle East'.

Begin also boasted that 'Israel needs no guarantees from any European nation to ensure its security'.[23]

In the US, Secretary of State Edmund Muskie praised the 'moderation of the European statement', and pointed out that the 'United States is not trying to keep the PLO out of a settlement in the Middle East, but Washington could not accept the PLO's entering the peace process as long as that organization has not given up demanding the destruction of Israel'. However, he did not rule out the possiblility of including PLO observers in the Egyptian delegation if the PLO responded to American expectations.[24]

In all, Arab reaction to the Venice statement was cautiously optimistic. Israel was absolutely rejectionist. The Carter Administration was timid about supporting a plan that might destroy the chances of survival of the Camp David process, which was already gasping for breath, and prevent the envisaged participation of the missing actor in the Camp David agreement, King Hussein of Jordan.[25]

In the three months following the Venice declaration, Gaston Thorn, the president of the EC Council of Ministers, undertook three fact-finding missions to the Middle East. The first, which began on 30 July 1980, with a visit to the headquarters of the League of Arab States in Tunis, took him to seven Arab Mashreq countries and to Israel. In Israel, he attempted to advance the EC peace plans as an 'alternative in the event of the Camp David agreement breaking down irretrievably'.[26]

In Lebanon, M. Thorn had a long discussion with Yasser Arafat, who said he was 'in favor of the European initiative'.[27] The PLO was also in favour of an amendment to UN Resolution 242 (of 1967) so that it would recognize the Palestinian right to a homeland.

The Lebanese Government, on the other hand—besieged by rumours that the Europeans were debating the incorporation of part of Lebanon with the West Bank of the Jordan to create a Palestinian state—strongly voiced the view that the Lebanese problem should be separately dealt with and not be associated with the Palestinian problem.[28] Whether the Europeans were discussing the possibility of ceding part of Lebanon to the Palestinians is a contention that could not be substantiated by our research and, at best, should be viewed merely as a rumour.

On a second visit to the area, starting on 1 September 1980,

Thorn visited Alexandria and talked with the then Egyptian President Anwar Sadat. His second planned visit to Israel and to the West Bank to meet with Arab leaders of the occupied territory had to be cancelled at the last minute—Israel was not interested in receiving the EC official in the West Bank area, since it would have encouraged the Palestinian political leadership there to voice its demands internationally. The official Israeli reason was their inability to assemble the West Bank leaders in Jerusalem in time to meet with M. Thorn.[29] The EC president, therefore, made a second attempt at the end of September when he succeeded in meeting with a number of West Bank leaders who expressed their strongest support for al Fatah and for the goal of a Palestinian state.[30]

Meanwhile, Spain and the Islamic bloc at the UN were pushing for a new peace plan. The Spanish peace plan, as it became known, was a four-part plan involving the holding of a special session of the UN Security Council which would aim at adopting a new resolution amending Resolution 242, and the holding of a major UN-sponsored conference involving all of the parties. The EC was not ready to support such a plan, however. In the opinion of Gaston Thorn, the EC's special representative to the UN Special Session of the General Assembly on the Palestinian problem, the new resolution would 'contradict' the earlier UN Resolution 242 through failure to offer 'necessary guarantees for the existence of Israel'.[31] The US threat to veto this resolution in the Security Council forced its draftees to submit it to the General Assembly, where it was adopted.[32]

At the specially convened session of the UN General Assembly in the summer of 1980, the EC countries abstained from voting on a resolution which called on the UN to convene a Middle East conference with the participation of all sides, including the PLO, and to establish a 'blue beret' UN force in occupied territories following an Israeli withdrawal to begin by 15 November 1980. The resolution, which was passed by 112 to 7 with 24 abstentions, marked for the first time in recent memory the Greek Government's alignment with the nine EC members in abstaining on a Middle East related resolution. The reasons offered by the Greek Foreign Minsiter at the UN session were similar to those of Gaston Thorn, who interrupted his Middle East trip to attend the UN session. The Greek representative claimed that the foreign policy of his government was committed to a Palestinian participation, but he viewed the resolution as 'not balanced', since it omitted guarantees for Israel.[33]

Europe: A Trusted Mediator

In seven years of active European diplomatic involvement in the Middle East, Europe has succeeded in speaking diplomatically with one voice. It has also cast a new political shadow in the region, differentiated from and independent of the US. The European peace plan, while short of Arab expectations, filled a void in American policy toward the region—a void stemming from the American preoccupation with presidential elections which, in effect, asked that the world be put on hold.

The independent and even-handed European stance toward the Palestinian question, while perhaps not durable or stable in the long run, might provide Europe with an opportunity to play the role of trusted mediator. The wavering in European diplomatic commitment toward the problem should not be viewed as intractable when the Community marshals the diplomatic strength to push its Venice peace plan directly and even, perhaps, with American support. Peace plans tend to be pruned in application. However, the European initiative did stimulate other *démarches* from the US and Spain, and even from some Arab states.

Recent developments on the European scene and the absence of any new comments regarding the Middle East in the European Council point to a lessening of European efforts toward finding a peaceful formula in the region. The electoral defeat of French President Valéry Giscard d'Estaing, a long-time supporter of the Arab world, has not only deprived the Arab world of traditional French support, but has dampened collective diplomatic activity in Europe itself. The French Foreign Minister, Claude Cheysson, former EC Commissioner for External Affairs, has, however, renewed his country's commitment to a Palestinian homeland. It is safe to say, therefore, that the Palestinian problem may have lost its former primacy on the diplomatic agenda of Europe, but it remains an important aspect of European relations with the Arab world.

On the other hand, there appears on the diplomatic horizon a bridging of the gap between the US and the Soviet Union (which traditionally has involved the context and participants of any future negotiations) for the convening of a multilateral conference on the Middle East under the aegis of the UN and with the full participation of the PLO and the Europeans. The agenda of the proposed conference, as rumoured, would include elements of the Venice declaration of June 1980 and the Spanish peace plan. The date of such a conference has not, however, been specified.[34]

Collective European pressure on Washington does, however, bring about some policy differentiation in Washington DC. European and Canadian pressure exerted during the recent Western economic summit meeting held in Ottawa, among other factors, succeeded in delaying the shipment of six US-built F16 jets to Israel.[35] This important contribution on the part of the Europeans toward lessening the level of Israeli violence in the region is directly attributable to the development of Euro–Arab channels of communication and amity which have evolved throughout the last seven years.

Notes

1. Winston Churchill's Fulton, Missouri, speech of 1947 is often cited as an example of the British intellectual contribution to the policy of the cold war. The German contribution to American foreign policy must also be noted, as in Willy Brandt's 1968 Ostpolitik policy, which signalled the onset of US–USSR détente.
2. See, for example, the interview with French President Mitterand in *Time* 29 June 1980). Even those Western European countries that are not dependent on the Arabs for oil, such as Norway, are adopting a positive view of the need for a Palestinian state. On Norway's support of a Palestinian homeland, see an interview with Norway's ambassador to the UN, Ole Algard, in *The New York Times* (5 June 1980).
3. Quoted in *Bulletin of the European Communities*, 6/11 (1973), p. 26-7.
4. *Keesing's Contemporary Archives*, 19 (26 November-2 December 1973), pp. 9-10.
5. 'Copenhagen Summit', *Bulletin of the European Communities*, 6/12 (1973), pp. 9-10.
6. See the Twenty-Ninth Session of the UN General Assembly, Resolution A/RES/3237.
7. See R. Stebbins and E. P. Adams (eds), *American Foreign Relations, 1973: A Documentary Record* (New York, New York University Press and the Council on Foreign Relations, 1976), p. 606.

8. *Bulletin of the European Communities*, 11/9 (1978), p. 109.
9. While the Europeans have been more attuned to Arab-sponsored resolutions, historically they have abstained from outright support of Arab-introduced resolutions at the UN General Assembly. However, in 1979 they began to change their pattern of abstention.
10. *Bulletin of the European Communities*, 11/9 (1978), p. 109.
11. Ibid.
12. See a full quotation of their Paris statement in Assembly of Western European Union, General Affairs Committee, Twenty-Fifth Ordinary Session, 'Western Security and the Middle East' (Brief prepared by Sir Frederic Bennet, rapporteur, Paris, December 1979), pp. 42-3.
13. Ibid., p. 43.
14. Ibid., p. 48.
15. Ibid., p. 49.
16. *Europe Political Day* (published by Agence Internationale d'Information pour la Presse, Luxembourg-Brussels), 2924 (9 June 1980).
17. *Europe Political Day*, 2927 (13 June 1980).
18. Ibid.
19. Ibid.
20. 'European Council on the Middle East' a document provided by the Washington DC office of the EC. See also, European Council, 'Declaration of the European Council on the Middle East', Venice, 12-13 June 1980, (released by the EC Information Office, Washington DC). For an analysis of the German initiative, see H. Sicherman, 'Politics of Dependence: Western Europe and the Arab-Israeli Conflict', *Orbis*, 23/4, (Winter 1980), 845-57; see particularly pp. 845-54.
21. *Europe Political Day*, 2929 (16 June 1980).
22. Ibid.
23. Ibid.
24. Ibid.
25. Ibid.
26. *Europe Political Day*, 2963 (25 August 1980).
27. Ibid.
28. Ibid.
29. *Europe Political Day*, 2978 (1 September 1980).
30. *Europe Political Day*, 2990 (21 October 1980).
31. See the Thorn address in *Bulletin of the European Communities*, 13, 7/8 (1980), p. 87.
32. *Europe Political Day*, 2957 (26 July 1980).
33. *Europe Political Day*, 2960 (31 July 1980); and UN General Assembly, Thirty-Fifth Session, 'Provisional Verbatim Record of the Sixth Meeting' (A35/PV.6, 23 September 1980).
34. The rumours of a UN-sponsored conference and President Reagan's

implied acceptance of it are based on Soviet President Leonid Brezhnev's speech to the Twenty-Sixth Congress of the CPSU on 23 February 1981, quoted in *Keesing's Contemporary Archives*, 27/18 (1 May 1980), p. 30837, as well as on some 'inside information' available to *Saudi Report* (Houston, Texas), 2/32 (18 May 1981), p. 2, which reported that the Reagan Administration 'has quietly given the green light' to UN Secretary-General Kurt Waldheim to pursue negotiations on the agenda and the time of the conference.

35. *Los Angeles Times* (21 July 1981), p. 1.

8 THE UNITED STATES AND EURO–ARAB ASSOCIATIVE DIPLOMACY

Inasmuch as associative diplomacy is reflected in increasing aid linkage structures between the Arab world and Europe, and inasmuch as these processes would bring the two regions closer together, then it is no wonder that they would not be favourably endorsed by the United States. As a nascent world power, a geo-political European influence in its peripheral area would certainly be interpreted as a lessening of the US role in those same regions.

The purpose of this chapter is to underline the political and economic role of the US in the Arab world *vis-à-vis* its European allies (and sometimes rivals). It does not purport to describe US foreign policy in the region, but will merely examine American views of various European Community (EC) policies, namely the Euro–Arab Dialogue, the EC's position regarding the Palestine Liberation Organization (PLO), and the bilateral agreements linking the EC to several Arab Mashreq and Mahgreb countries.

Economically, the US has attempted since the oil disruption of 1973 to maintain the position of leader of the Western alliance and to extend this leadership from the strategic sphere to economic areas such as energy. The US response to the 1973 oil embargo was largely bureaucratic, through the creation of a new International Energy Administration (IEA) to counterbalance the weight of the Organization of Petroleum Exporting Countries (OPEC). European responses, however, have largely been typified by bilateral agreements with oil producers and by regionally based dialogues such as the Euro–Arab Dialogue.

Professing to abhor bilateral deals, the Nixon Administration worked to line up the club of rich oil consumers in the IEA.[1] EC response to the IEA was not initially favourable, since it felt that the new institution would rob the Community of another opportunity to define its own policy and since Washington, through the IEA, would move the decision-making focus away from Brussels. It is no wonder that Michel Jobert, the French Foreign Minister at the time, was echoing French national attitudes and Community sentiment when, at a Washington energy conference on 11 February 1974, he characterized the new agency as an attempt to 'impose a new world energy order'.[2] While the original aim of the agency was a disguised challenge to OPEC, nevertheless its stated constitution did not exclude any future negotiations and dialogue with these oil producers. And while the Community response was regional in character, embodying most Arab states, rich and poor, the US preferred to negotiate if necessary in functional terms with only the oil-supplying Arab states, and to address specific issues of supply, security, and payments. Such an approach is in tune with the US aversion to regional politics (except in military terms) and its predilection to view the world as made up of nation states rather than of political or economic blocs. This suspicion of political and economic amalgamation, particularly as applied to the Third World, reflects a global power's bargaining-induced preferences for dealing with individual states, and perhaps even embraces traces of the old American diplomatic ethos that linked bloc politics to instability and conflict.[3]

It is no wonder that Europe has been more successful in creating trade blocs by bringing former colonies into a web of associative diplomacy, as fully expressed in the Lomé Conventin. There is no American counterpart to the Lomé Convention in its foreign economic relations since the decline of the cold war. This distinction between what Jagdish Baghwati calls 'benign intent' on the part of the EC and 'benign neglect' on the part of the US is an important distinction in describing the economic policies of the two entities toward the Arab world.[4]

'Benign intent' is, to Baghwati, a euphemism for active European support and development assistance to the under-developed countries of the world. 'Benign neglect' is the assertion that the underdeveloped countries of the world can fend for themselves without the active transfer of funds from the North and with little official intervention in the workings of the inter-national marketplace. It is essentially a policy of content economic power, like that of the US.

US reliance on an open international marketplace and its criticism of the Europeans' rush for bilateral agreements with

the Arab oil states did not prevent the US itself from approach-
ing the Arab states through the same modalities of bilateral
commissions, the first of which was established with Saudi
Arabia in 1974. Since then the US seems also to have fostered
this policy path for other strategic purposes with three other
Arab states, Egypt, Jordan, and Tunisia, as well as with Israel.[5]

The divergence in appropriate approaches toward the Arab
world and the responses to the energy crisis have been epitom-
ized in the US views of the ongoing Euro–Arab Dialogue. In so
far as the US could feel the developing commonalities of shared
interest between Europe and the Arab world, through the
mechanism of the Euro–Arab Dialogue, it decided to offer an
alternative dialogue in which its own leadership would be
solidified.

US Secretary of State Henry Kissinger went on record in
1973 and 1974 as asserting the primacy of a US-led dialogue
as the only path to co-operation with the Arab oil producers.
He stated:

A well-conceived producer–consumer meeting in which the consumers
do not seek selfish advantages either as a group or individually, far from
leading to confrontation could, instead, lay the basis of a new co-operative relationship. But it will do so only if it is well-prepared and if the
consumers have first constructed a solid basis of cooperation among
themselves.[6]

The US stance on the Euro–Arab Dialogue as a form of
European associative diplomacy is well known. In March 1974
the EC Council of Ministers adopted a policy proposal to the
League of Arab States for the beginning of a wide-ranging discussion of aid and trade between the two regions. US response
was swift and negative. The following day, 5 March, George S.
Vest, a spokesman for the US Department of State, expressed
some displeasure over the Community proposal, claiming that
'the United States was not consulted on that particular activity.
It was informed about it after it became public.'[7] In the ensuing
crisis that developed between Washington and its European
allies over the issue, which was purportedly lack of consultation, Kissinger attacked the European allies for what he called
'self-assertiveness and the seeming victory that they are striving
for'.[8] A few days later, the zenith of the crisis over the Euro–
Arab Dialogue was reached when President Nixon warned the

Common Market countries not to 'gang up against the United States' in political and economic areas or they would face a reduction in the level of US troops stationed in Europe.[9]

Kissinger and succeeding US secretaries of state have argued on many occasions that neither Europe nor the US could single-handedly meet the challenge of the world oil producers.[10] This continuous whipping up of oil consumers' sentiments can only be perceived as a method of keeping the Europeans from seeking their own oil-supply accommodation with the Arab states, except through the aegis of the US—a policy which ensures continuous satellite status for the EC member countries.

Kissinger, more than any other American secretary of state, laboured to keep the Europeans from attaining some form of oil-based concordance with the Arab states. This effort at times necessitated the personal dispatch of high-ranking US officials to both Europe and the Arab world to dissuade them from any oil agreement that might be achieved to the exclusion of the US. On the eve of the Abu Dhabi meeting of the Euro–Arab Dialogue (27 November 1975), Secretary of State Kissinger sent his special envoy, Gerald Parsky, then Assistant Secretary of the Treasury, to persuade the Arab oil producers in the Gulf to delete the issue of oil supply and security from the agenda of the dialogue. He was successful in accomplishing this, but such a diplomatic intervention earned him resentment in Community institutions.[11]

The US and the Political Dimension of Euro–Arab Associative Diplomacy

Whereas the prevailing view in the EC circles in post-1973 period has been to work for a peaceful resolution of the Palestinian question through an even-handed approach to all parties, American policy has tended to 'pacify' the Middle East through some form of political settlement. The vernacularly similar words may be used journalistically as synonyms, but they nevertheless convey different political connotations. Peace can be taken to mean the reaching of some form of political equilibrium through bargaining and negotiation, and peaceful settlement is the advancement of an acceptable formula, perhaps through some coercion, for ending a conflict without war but not necessarily resulting in a political equilibrium.

The use of different terms also reflects other points of departure between the EC stance, as provided for in the Venice declaration of June 1980 (see Appendix B), and US foreign policy. For the EC, Palestinian participation in any negotiations with Israel is highly imperative if peace is to come to the Holy Land. For the US, the Palestinians are only a single part of a state-to-state conflict. To use the metaphor of Peter Jay, former British ambassador to the US, the Palestinian 'shoe' would not necessarily have been made to drop in the Camp David accords.[12]

Although it is not the intention of this study to engage in a full analysis of American foreign policy toward the Palestinian problem or the Camp David agreement, it suffices to illustrate the negative commitment of the US to exclude the Palestine Liberation Organization (PLO) from the peace process as a form of appeasement of Israeli leaders, for obvious US internal political exigencies. The EC has indicated on many occasions that the 'association' of the PLO is a necessary requisite for peace in the region. The US has refused to deal with the PLO (except clandestinely) until the PLO accepts the existence of the state of Israel, thus pre-empting what would have been the core of any future negotiation, if it is ever achieved, between the PLO and Israel.[13]

Furthermore, Israeli lobbying efforts in the US Congress surpass any comparable efforts in European parliaments, while at the same time, little pro-Arab sentiment is depicted in the European Parliament resolutions on the Middle East. Nevertheless, we can see a proliferation of Euro–Arab parliamentary groups at the national level, something unheard of in the halls of the US Congress since, for all intents and purposes, that institution considers Israel to be the only democratic state in the Middle East.

While the US Government has imposed upon itself the prohibition of any public contact with the PLO, it has also worked to stave off any attempt by the European Political Co-operation System to extend a *de jure* recognition to the PLO. On 30 May 1980 US Secretary of State Edwin Muskie intervened personally with France and Germany to thwart any attempt to extend *de jure* recognition to the PLO by the EC member states,[14] lest the US reduce its level of troops stationed in Europe.

Whether these and other developments will bring about a major shift in the US approach to Israel and the PLO, or whether they are merely an aberration, cannot be determined at this juncture. There may develop a scenario in which, at a time of waning French support to the Palestinians, the Regan Administration might fill this policy void. One cannot, however, be overly optimistic and expect long-standing policies to be changed overnight. The Arab states must work and earn the backing of international power brokers in Washington and in European capitals.[15]

The US and the European Mediterranean Policy

The EC's Common Agricultural Policy (CAP) and its associated systems of artificial prices and barriers to trade have, for a long time, been a major point of contention in US–EC agricultural trade. The fact that after 1975 the EC began to lower the tariff rates for the produce of several African countries, first for those in the Lomé Convention and later also for some Arab Mediterranean countries, did not find favour with Washington. The matrix of associative diplomacy that was seen to develop between the Community and its African and Mediterranean partners was viewed in Washington as an anathema to the spirit of free trade, symbolized by the General Agreement on Tariffs and Trade (GATT), and the US fought within the GATT in negotiations in 1977 and 1978 to abolish some of the Community's import policies.[16]

Since the countries of the Mediterranean, both Arab and non-Arab, are largely agricultural countries, the new ties were seen as 'irritants' to American agricultural interests. By 1978, more and more US citrus producers were forced to divert their exports from Community markets and seek new outlets in the thriving Arab Gulf markets. The Community share of US fruit exports (Table 8.1) had declined from about 2 per cent in 1975 to 1.5 per cent in 1979. Similarly, its share of vegetable exports from the US had declined from 2.73 per cent in 1976 to 1.39 per cent in 1979. These facts generated a strong complaint from the US, first lodged with a specially convened GATT panel in February 1978.[17] The US was irritated by the pricing policies of the Community which, on the one hand, extended some quota preferences to Mediterranean and African produce, to

Table 8.1. Value of United States Exports of Fruits and Vegetables to the European Community Market (1975–1980)

Year	Fruits		Vegetables	
	$US millions	*as % of total US exports*	*$US millions*	*as % of total US exports*
1975	43,660	2.05	70,809	1.40
1976	149,376	1.93	184,115	2.73
1977	160,636	1.93	125,239	1.98
1978	170,201	1.68	101,488	1.44
1979	169,359	1.50	106,368	1.39
1980	265,760	1.99	148,367	1.24

Source: Raw data derived from *Foreign Agricultural Trade of the United States (FATUS)* (Washington DC, US Department of Agriculture, Economics and Statistics Service, May–June 1981), Table 8, pp. 40, 49.

the exclusion of US farm exporters and, on the other hand, subsidized EC farm exports to Third World countries.

The subject was even brought to the attention of the Bonn economic summit conference of 17 July 1978, which adopted a proclamation stating that the 'uniform application of the GATT rules is vital', which meant that the Community could not use escape clauses in the GATT, such as Article 15 which allows members of the organization to extend preferential treatment for the purposes of reconstruction and economic development.[18]

US pressure, therefore, succeeded in allowing more American agricultural produce into European markets. Table 8.1 shows that the lean years for American exporters of fruits may have ended in 1980, and even early 1981 statistics show a measurable turn-round in the export picture.

The question remains, however, of whether the Community's Mediterranean policy was responsible for the waning of US fruit and vegetable exports to the Community in the period 1975–9, or whether this development was mainly due to internal constraints imposed through the CAP. The answer is not a simple one. There is no doubt that Spain, Morocco, and Israel, the three largest citrus producers in the Mediterranean region, may have effectively hindered US exports. While the author is not an authority on agricultural economy, a very tentative measure of the size of this hindrance based on available data covering the five-year period is suggested here.

The Community's agricultural trade with the Mediterranean countries, which are not entirely Arab, may be said to have hurt US fruit and fruit preparation exports by something in the order of 1.4 per cent per year. US vegetable and vegetable preparation exports to the Community may have suffered a further injury of 3.2 per cent per year.[19] These estimates are based on a comparison of the rates of increase/decrease of US agricultural exports to the EC with the rates of increase in total US agricultural exports over the same period.

At this juncture it is interesting to note that, as both Japan and the EC continuously impose certain restrictions in the face of US agricultural products to help their own farmers, more and more citrus and vegetable growers and canners are turning to the burgeoning countries of the Arab Gulf for export relief. Due to lack of adequate internal produce to satisfy increasing demands and to import subsidies, particularly on food imports, Saudi Arabia became in 1980 the third largest importer of US canned vegetable goods and, with the United Arab Emirates, has equalled the former importance of the EC for US citrus exports.[20]

Notes

1. Kissinger compared the European scramble for oil in 1973 to the 'beggar thy neighbor' policies of the late 1930s. See his speech at the Washington Energy Conference in *Vital Speeches of the Day*, 40/11 (15 March 1974), p. 323.
2. See the full text of M. Jobert's speech, ibid., 325-7.
3. See former US ambassador to the EC Isaiah Frank's paper on 'Responses of the United States to New Tensions in North-South Relations', in G. Douglass (ed.), *The New Interdependence: The European Community and the United States* (Lexington, Mass., Lexington Books, D. C. Heath, 1979), pp. 113-19.
4. J. Baghwati (ed.), *The New International Economic Order: The North-South Debate* (Cambridge, Mass., MIT Press, 1977).
5. S. D. Hayes, 'Joint Economic Commissions as Instruments of U.S. Foreign Policy', *Middle East Journal* 31/1, 16-30. Also, C. F. Bergsten, 'U.S.-Saudi Economic Interests', *Vital Speeches of the Day*, 46/13 (15 April 1980), 400-5.
6. See Kissinger's speech at the Washington Energy Conference in op. cit., p. 324.

7. *The New York Times* (6 March 1974), p. 1.
8. *Idem* (12 March 1974), p. 3.
9. *Idem* (16 March 1974), p. 1.
10. Compare, for example, the speech delivered by Dr Kissinger to The Pilgrims, a British-American friendship organization, London, 12 December 1973, and Secretary of State Muskie's speech to the Commonwealth Club of San Francisco, repeating the same theme, seven years later, in *Vital Speeches of the Day*, 39/24 (15 December 1973), 166-9, and *Current Policy*, 209 (8 August 1980).
11. Based on personal interviews held at the offices of the EC Commission and the Council of the European Community, Brussels, November-December 1980.
12. Although Ambassador Jay is critical of the Community and of the PLO, he seems to doubt the American commitment to the other half of the Camp David agreement, namely the Palestinian autonomy plan. See his article 'Regionalism as Geopolitics', *Foreign Affairs, America, and the World*, 58/3, (1979) 485-514.
13. For an overview of covert US contacts with the PLO since 1975, see a three-part series on the PLO in the *Los Angeles Times* (21, 23, 25 June 1981).
14. *The New York Times* (31 May 1980), p. 1.
15. *Los Angeles Times* (20 July 1981), p. 15; *Time* (27 July 1981), p. 23.
16. See the report of the GATT panel on this problem in *Basic Instruments and Selected Documents*, 25th Supplement: *Protocols, Decisions, Reports, 1977 and 1979* and *Thirty-Fourth Session*, (Geneva, GATT, January 1979), pp. 68-107. See also a three-part report by Omero Sabatini, leader of the European Community Group, Trade Operations Division, Foreign Agricultural Service, US Department of Agriculture, 'The European Community and Its Special Third-Country Partnership', *Foreign Agriculture* (21 and 28 February and 7 March 1977).
17. See Sabatini and A. Bailey, 'European Community Mediterranean Proposals Point to Higher Import Charges', *Foreign Agriculture* (20 February 1978), p. 13.
18. See the text of the Bonn summit declaration in *Historic Documents of 1978* (Washington DC, US Congressional Quarterly Inc., February 1979), pp. 535-42; see especially p. 542.
19. Our calculation is based on averaging the annual differences in the percentages of US exports of a given commodity to total US exports of that commodity in the given year for a given region, as they appear in Table 8.1 of this study. The difference is, therefore, based not merely on actual variation of exports but also reflects losses of potential exports that may have occurred in the absence of the Community's Mediterranean policy.

20. See US Department of Agriculture, *US Foreign Agriculture Trade Statistical Report, Calendar Year 1980* (A 105, 1412: 980, Washington DC, US Government Printing Office, May 1981), Tables 11 and 15.

9   SUMMARY AND CONCLUSIONS

This study of European associative diplomacy toward the Arab world has been an examination, from both the theoretical and the empiricial perspectives, of the conduct of a concatenated foreign policy by a regional organization.

From the theoretical perspective, the underlying economic bases of regional policies have been demonstrated. The European Community (EC), which is primarily an economic institution, has shaped its policies toward the Arab region within an economic context. An example of this was the establishment of regional programmes of development assistance in the Arab world. For the Arab world, it was foreseen that an emerging structure of European associative diplomacy would inevitably produce political and diplomatic gains for the Arab states.

Economic dependence between the two regions has been presented here as one (but not the only one) of the most effective ways by which the Europeans could voice regional policy—termed associative diplomacy. It has been demonstrated that this form of diplomacy was tempered by both internal and external factors. Once the process of associative diplomacy was embarked upon, it seemed to give new impetus to the concept of a united Europe. New institutional arrangements in the European Political Co-operation System (EPCS) were formed to accomplish new tasks. The EPCS worked to support both the EC Commission and the EC Council of Ministers in organizing the meetings and activities of the Euro–Arab Dialogue (EAD). The image of a European Community active on the world scene has also been enhanced by the European Middle East peace initiative, which was advanced through the resolutions and statements of European summit meetings. Thus, on such concrete foreign policy issues as the EAD and the Middle East crisis, the Community and the EPCS worked in unison to give meaning and credence to the Community's associative diplomacy processes.

In examining the structure and processes of European associative diplomacy, we have found that the least publicized activities of this form of diplomacy have been the most successful. The co-financing efforts between Arab and European groups have generated approximately $700 million in development aid to African countries. Although that sum is not massive, given the dire need for development assistance in that area, it remains an important contribution to overall EC aid commitments within the Lomé agreements, and in 1980 alone provided 20 per cent of the budget for projects under these agreements.

The urgency of the EAD has reflected the availability of oil. During crisis periods, such as early 1974 and again during the Iranian crisis of 1979–80, the EAD seemed to take on new urgency and, conversely, that urgency diminished during those periods when oil supplies were more plentiful. On the whole, the EAD has failed to live up to original expectations for providing a grand design for Arab economic development, nor has it provided the Europeans with any measurable assurance of secure oil supplies. Nevertheless, the EAD has provided diplomatic impetus for European business firms to enter the lucrative construction markets in the Arab Gulf states. It has also resulted in a new feeling of amity between Arab and European regional decision makers.

As to the Palestinian question and possible European recognition of the Palestine Liberation Organization (PLO), the Arab states have collectively succeeded in influencing the Europeans to the point where there is now a significant difference between the political strategies adopted in European capitals and those in Washington. A year ago, the Europeans extended quasi-recognition to the PLO and have, for years, maintained direct and public contacts with the PLO leadership. The evolution of the European stance on the Palestinian question may, therefore, have helped the image of Europe in the Arab world and may have enhanced the possibility for the further development of associative diplomacy.

The EAD has reflected the need of each regional organization to provide its members with political and economic security. For the EC, the continuous and stable flow of the strategic Arab commodity of oil has been the most pressing need. For the League of Arab States, European diplomatic backing in peace negotiations has been highly sought. While the two goals may have been lofty, the two organizations have met the minimal requisites of their stated objectives.

For the PLO, the EAD has been a successful exercise in symbolic politics. Through the EAD, the PLO has succeeded in specifically addressing the Europeans, and engaged in a successful effort to secure international diplomatic recognition of Palestinian representation. Through the dialogue, the PLO has transformed itself from an Arab regional factor to an international force that must be addressed in any differentiation of Middle Eastern political calculuses.

Associative diplomacy has imbued the EC institutions with a new legitimacy with which to expand the scope of EC bilateral agreements with Arab states. The Community sought to expand the number of these bilateral links from seven to ten or twelve agreements, mainly with the small states of the Arab Peninsula. Through these proposed agreements, the Community may have hoped to speak to neighbouring rich countries and thus to influence their monetary and pricing policies.

In this study, the objective was to determine the theoretical meaning of European associative diplomacy through the investigation of a set of five hypotheses. Associative diplomacy has been examined within the limits of those propositions.

The first hypothesis sought to establish the existence of a discernible European regional dependence on the Arab world through an examination of the types and volume of European imports of certain strategic goods and commodities from the Arab world. Our research showed a declining dependence by Europe on Arab oil imports, ranging from 60.5 per cent in 1972 to 42 per cent in 1981.[1] The period 1970–3 was the period of greatest dependence.

In examining the pattern of historical dependence and correlating it with the aid policies of the European powers (the members of the EC) over the period 1961–77, we found a strong correlation between European aid and the price of Arab oil exports. However, only a small correlation was found to exist between European aid and the price of non-strategic Arab raw materials, suggesting, perhaps, that European regional concern for dependence is confined to petroleum. Other Arab raw materials are either not particularly important for the Europeans or the EC is dependent on imports of these materials from other international regions. Thus, our second hypothesis is only partially correct.

The third hypothesis proposed that a linkage exists between the level of intensity of dependence by the EC and the urgency of its overtures to and dialogues with the Arab world. In an examination of the EAD, the tendency of the dialogue to reflect the ebb and flow of oil supply has been apparent. It is, therefore, no coincidence that the EAD, which had been allowed to lapse after the Camp David accord, was revived only after the 1979 Iranian revolution and the ensuing oil crisis.

In examining relations between the EC and the Arab resource-poor states and the Arab oil-producing states, we approximated the conditions of our next hypothesis. Inferences from the correlates of European aid, coupled with the fact that trade issues that arose in bilateral negotiations were transferred by some Arab states (without much success) to the EAD, suggest that this hypothesis (the tendency of the Community to influence the Arab region) may be true. The size of Euro–Arab co-financing efforts in the Mahgreb countries, Egypt, and the African–Arab countries also provides partial evidence in support of this hypothesis.

Finally, this entire study has proved our contention that EC overtures and dialogues tend to be moulded into a permanent pattern of associative diplomacy, provided that conditions of regional dependence continue to be equally maintained. Recognition by negotiators in the EAD of the saliency of this triad may have helped in the transfer of bilateral gains into multilateral benefits. An example of this was the agreement within the EAD on the rights and privileges of guest workers only after such a declaration had already been incorporated into the 1976 bilateral agreements between the EC and the Arab Mahgreb countries.

The concept of a foreign policy for a regional institution is a fascinating topic of study. Regional organizations are necessarily created to serve common regional needs and interests. The fact that the EC chose, both by change and in response to pressure, to extend its activities into an area beyond its own geographical boundaries without a constitutional crisis of the like of 1966 is an unprecedented feat.[2]

While this study has merely shed some light on European

associative diplomacy toward the Arab world, other similar areas for research may be found in EC relations with the Asian countries or Africa. Researchers could examine other types of regional dependence that impel other regional organizations to pursue similar policies of associative diplomacy, for example, the policy of the League of Arab States *vis à vis* the African countries and the Organization of African Unity.

Researchers in international relations should, in future, look at the pattern of dependence by entire regions rather than by single states, for such patterns of dependence may be correlated with the processes of associative diplomacy. The task of the analyst should be to look beyond an examination of regional economic dependence to other facets—cultural or religious dependence, for example. The subject of regional dependence is as far-ranging and as varied as the perspectives and imaginations of the students of international regional politics.

Notes

1. Commission of the European Communities, Directorate-General for Economic and Financial Affairs, *European Economy*, No. 8 (March 1981), Table 22; *idem*, 4 (November 1979), p. 82.
2. This 1966 constitutional crisis, which lasted from 2 July 1965, to 29 January 1966, and which resulted in a French boycott of the meetings of the Community for seven months, was over the financing of the CAP and the role of the Commission in the formulation and deliberation of issues and decisions in the EC Council of Ministers.

APPENDIX A: SUPPORTING DATA: EUROPEAN COMMUNITY IMPORTS/EXPORTS FROM/TO THE ARAB WORLD

Table A.1. European Community Imports from the Arab World* (1961–70) (in $US millions)

Country	1961	1962	1963	1964	1965	1966	1967	1968	1969	1970
Algeria	689.2	783	677.1	725.5	716.13	765.5	759.6	878.1	940	967.2
Bahrain	83.4	59.7	54.2	46.8	18.9	23.5	42.9	48.3	24.6	27.77
Egypt	98.4	124.7	136.8	145	128.3	119.2	111.9	152.2	181.07	235.15
Iraq	548	578.7	645.1	626.1	611.3	597.5	545.9	776.5	789.2	729.03
Jordan	0.9	1.7	1.8	4.4	3.6	3.3	4.3	1.2	1.5	1.6
Kuwait	903.2	954.1	1,005.3	1,076.1	942.8	941.3	999.5	1,490	1,277.13	1,358.6
Lebanon	63.2	83.3	74	104.8	63.5	108.9	45.6	1,058	99.48	77.79
Libya	67.8	132.7	344.9	622.8	879.9	956.7	1,112.0	2,103.7	2,363.52	2,626
Mauritania	1	1.1	13.9	54	69.5	77.9	77.4	94.5	106.4	104.6
Morocco	309.7	315.6	344.8	376.5	384.5	368.9	347.2	375.8	421.51	451.43
Oman	–	0.2	1	33.7	93.9	128.4	209.2	375.4	344.96	375.84
Qatar	49.4	88.1	70.2	80.5	67.5	116.8	135.3	267.3	233.4	259.4
Saudi Arabia	301	288.1	299.1	399.7	502.2	780.8	826.9	1,033.5	1,215.41	1,557.84
Somalia	20.1	18.4	23	16.3	26.5	10.6	16	15.3	16.2	16.27
Sudan	83.4	101.3	110.6	96.1	97.8	97	98.8	135.2	128.43	128.11
Syria	131.5	154	150.5	122.9	124.5	96.5	77.3	84.3	76.88	99.04
Tunisia	137.7	164.3	166.4	138.3	106.6	115.5	111.3	116.6	123.1	127.49
UAE	–	3.2	31.6	76	62	–	–	248.5	229.6	281.1
Yemen	2	1.9	1.7	2.1	2.1	2.7	1	0	1.23	4.7
South Yemen	23.5	39.6	41.9	46.4	48.6	47.8	43.2	21.4	45.8	20.26
TOTAL	3,513.8	3,893.7	4,193.9	4,792	4,950.13	5,268.8	5,565.3	8,188.40	8,619.43	9,478.86
Extra-EC Imports	28,970	30,832	33,429	37,571	39,367	41,665	42,623	43,817.2	47,906.8	53,325.31
Per cent †	12.13	12.63	12.55	12.75	12.57	12.65	13.06	18.68	18.37	17.77

* Includes the United Kingdom and Denmark and excludes Jibuti.
† EC imports from the Arab world as a percentage of total EC imports.
Source: International Monetary Fund *Direction of Trade Statistics Annuals* (Washington DC, IMF, issues 1962–71).

Table A.2. European Community Imports from the Arab World* (1971–1979) (in $US millions)

Country	1971	1972	1973	1974	1975	1976	1977	1978	1979
Algeria	697	866	1,320	2,525	2,523	2,414	2,384	2,561	3,832
Bahrain	24	27	45	92	77	81	41	125	96
Egypt	208	158	236	337	406	757	808	1,250	1,976
Iraq	891	763	1,168	3,052	3,432	3,917	4,663	5,776	8,098
Jordan	1	2	1	5	10	13	13	26	31
Kuwait	1,664	1,812	2,047	3,698	3,006	2,683	3,081	3,659	6,005
Lebanon	94	99	171	295	84	53	49	46	66
Libya	2,272	1,894	2,440	5,521	3,230	4,487	4,412	4,170	6,704
Mauritania	92	105	113	146	158	146	148	108	169
Morocco	400	488	712	1,091	1,008	946	966	1,090	1,417
Oman	458	159	134	413	465	422	167	254	223
Qatar	262	322	477	1,031	902	1,377	954	961	1,210
Saudi Arabia	2,162	2,983	4,569	12,731	11,229	13,285	14,609	12,640	19,295
Somalia	11	15	14	18	13	19	20	19	35
Sudan	100	108	163	178	214	249	248	272	239
Syria	114	87	137	337	576	731	692	650	842
Tunisia	139	216	236	506	441	460	651	738	1,096
UAE	115	518	903	2,629	2,927	3,283	3,509	3,217	4,171
Yemen	1	4	4	6	3	10	4	18	12
South Yemen	28	8	20	25	9	6	10	29	64
TOTAL	9,733	10,634	14,910	34,636	30,713	35,339	37,429	37,611	55,581
Extra-EC Imports	63,506	72,946	103,666	156,178	155,600	178,429	195,980	227,324	298,968
Per cent †	15.33	14.58	14.38	22.18	19.74	19.81	19.10	16.55	18.59

For notes see Table A.1.

Table A.3. European Community Exports to the Arab World (1970–1980)* (in current $US millions)

Country	1970	1971	1972	1973	1974	1975	1976	1977	1978	1979	1980
Algeria	856.71	941	1,159	1,639	2,480	3,516	3,102	4,213	4,684	5,287	6,600
Bahrain	77.98	148	126	157	136	224	312	337	402	447	458
Egypt	330.9	365	366	568	1,008	1,705	1,753	2,000	2,417	3,285	4,439
Iraq	161.98	254	318	348	956	2,325	2,243	2,044	2,486	3,702	5,346
Jordan	61.32	92	107	136	169	276	476	443	522	765	995
Kuwait	231.09	329	328	395	525	742	1,124	1,434	1,679	1,888	2,089
Lebanon	286.75	438	549	711	965	804	186	715	811	1,201	1,517
Libya	310.1	518	851	1,265	2,033	2,578	2,503	3,075	3,463	4,814	5,938
Mauritania	25.92	28	46	62	83	133	122	153	121	141	182
Morocco	375.98	426	456	667	942	1,297	1,473	1,760	1,709	2,304	2,064
Oman	123.43	193	183	147	211	398	328	437	393	524	551
Qatar	28.8	95	93	132	109	236	343	438	462	579	559
Saudi Arabia	266.9	396	492	674	1,059	1,844	3,535	5,347	7,427	8,994	10,383
Somalia	20.71	30	63	63	66	76	57	140	178	230	298
Sudan	85.61	141	172	221	222	371	469	555	715	572	667
Syria	91.12	150	199	296	582	756	1,189	1,005	1,047	1,490	1,799
Tunisia	186.25	230	325	449	674	913	948	1,124	1,453	1,704	2,165
UAE	58.9	132	200	429	490	956	1,322	1,777	2,066	2,475	2,900
Yemen	24.5	30	38	54	53	77	148	226	348	426	500
South Yemen	26.92	40	33	39	42	37	76	124	164	144	205
TOTAL	3,631.87	4,976	6,104	8,452	12,795	19,264	21,709	27,347	32,447	40,971	49,650
Extra-EC Exports	63,172.33	82,250	94,773	125,755	136,273	150,431	158,070	187,410	222,656	265,767	313,579
Per cent †	5.75	6.05	6.44	6.72	9.39	12.81	13.73	14.59	14.57	15.42	15.83

* Includes the United Kingdom and Denmark and excludes Jibuti.
† EC exports to the Arab world as a percentage of total extra-EC exports.
Source: International Monetary Fund, *Direction of Trade Statistics Annuals* (Washington DC, IMF, issues 1971–81).

APPENDIX B DECLARATION OF THE EUROPEAN COUNCIL ON THE MIDDLE EAST*

Venice, 13 June 1980

(1) The Heads of State and Government and the Ministers of Foreign Affairs held a comprehensive exchange of views on all aspects of the present situation in the Middle East, including the state of negotiations resulting from the agreements signed between Egypt and Israel in March 1979. They agreed that growing tensions affecting this region constitute a serious danger and render a comprehensive solution to the Israeli–Arab conflict more necessary and pressing than ever.

(2) The nine Member States of the European Community consider that the traditional ties and common interests which link Europe to the Middle East oblige them to play a special role and now require them to work in a more concrete way towards peace.

(3) In this regard, the nine countries of the Community based themselves on Security Council Resolutions 242 and 338 and the positions which they have expressed on several occasions, notably in their Declarations on 29 June 1977, 19 September 1978, 26 March and 18 June 1979, as well as in the speech made on their behalf on 25 September 1979 by the Irish Minister of Foreign Affairs at the 34th United Nations General Assembly.

(4) On the bases thus set out, the time has come to promote the recognition and implementation of the two principles universally accepted by the international community: the right to existence and to security of all the States in the region, including Israel, and justice for all the peoples, which implies the recognition of the legitimate rights of the Palestinian people.

(5) All of the countries in the area are entitled to live in peace within secure, recognized and guaranteed borders. The necessary guarantees for a peace settlement should be provided by the UN by a decision of the Security Council and, if necessary, on the basis of other mutually agreed procedures. The Nine declare that they are prepared to participate within the framework of a comprehensive settlement in a system

---

* Distributed by the EC Information Office, Washington DC.

of concrete and binding international guarantees, including [guarantees] on the ground.

(6) A just solution must finally be found to the Palestinian problem, which is not simply one of refugees. The Palestinian people, which is conscious of existing as such, must be placed in a position, by an appropriate process defined within the framework of the comprehensive peace settlement, to exercise fully its right to self-determination.

(7) The achievement of these objectives requires the involvement and support of all the parties concerned in the peace settlement which the Nine are endeavouring to promote in keeping with the principles formulated in the declaration referred to above. These principles apply to all the parties concerned, and thus to the Palestinian people, and to the PLO, which will have to be associated with the negotiations.

(8) The Nine recognize the special importance of the role played by the question of Jerusalem for all the parties concerned. The Nine stress that they will not accept any unilateral initiative designed to change the status of Jerusalem and that any agreement on the city's status should guarantee freedom of access for everyone to the Holy Places.

(9) The Nine stress the need for Israel to put an end to the territorial occupation which it has maintained since the conflict of 1967, as it has done for part of Sinai. They are deeply convinced that the Israeli settlements constitute a serious obstacle to the peace process in the Middle East. The Nine consider that these settlements, as well as modifications in population and property in the occupied Arab territories, are illegal under international law.

(10) Concerned as they are to put an end to violence, the Nine consider that only the renunciation of force or the threatened use of force by all the parties can create a climate of confidence in the area, and constitute a basic element for a comprehensive settlement of the conflict in the Middle East.

(11) The Nine have decided to make the necessary contacts with all the parties concerned. The objective of these contacts would be to ascertain the position of the various parties with respect to the principles set out in this declaration and in the light of the results of this consultation process to determine the form which such an initiative on their part could take.

BIBLIOGRAPHY

I. Books

A. S. al-Dajani, *al-Hiwar al-Arabi el-Urubbi, Wijhat Nazar Arabiyah wah-Wathaiq* [The Euro–Arab Dialogue: an Arab Viewpoint and Documents] (Beirut and Cairo, Anglo-Egyptian Library, 1976, in Arabic).

al-Dajani, *The Palestine Liberation Organization and the Euro–Arab Dialogue: A Study of the Political Aspect of the Dialogue and Documents* (Beirut, PLO, Research Centre, 1976, in Arabic).

H. Alker *et al.*, *Analyzing Global Interdependence* (Cambridge, Mass., MIT Press, 1974).

M. Ahmad, *Indo-Arab Relations* (Bombay, Popular Prakashan for the Indian Council for Cultural Relations in New Delhi, 1969).

S. Amin, *Accumulation on a World Scale: A Critique of the Theory of Underdevelopment* (New York, Monthly Review Press, 1974).

Amin, *Unequal Development: Social Formations at the Periphery of the Capitalist System* (New York, Monthly Review Press, 1976).

W. G. Barnes, *Europe and the Developing World, Association Under Part IV of the Treaty of Rome* (London, Chatham House European Series No. 2, February 1976).

C. F. Bergsten, *The Future of the International Economic Order: An Agenda for Research* (Lexington, Mass., Lexington Books, 1973).

A. Buchan, *Change Without War: The Shifting Structures of World Power* (New York, St. Martin's Press, 1975).

Lord Campbell of Eskan *et al.*, *Britain, the EEC and the Third World* (London, Overseas Development Institute and Praeger, 1972).

G. P. Casadio, *The Economic Challenge of the Arabs* (Westmead, England, Saxon House, 1976).

W. Chattick (ed.), *The Analysis of Foreign Policy Outputs* (Columbus, Ohio, Charles Merrill, 1974).

R. V. Cooper, *The Additionality Factor in U.S. Development Assistance* (R-984-Aid, Santa Monica, Cal., Rand Corporation, June 1972).

R. Cox and H. Jacobson (eds), *The Anatomy of Influence: Decision-Making in International Organizations* (New Haven, Yale University Press, 1974).

S. Demir, *Arab Development Funds in the Middle East* (New York, Pergamon Press for UNITAR, 1979).

G. Douglass (ed.), *The New Interdependence. The European Community and the United States* (Lexington, Mass., Lexington Books, D. C. Heath 1979).

M. East *et al., Why Nations Act* (Beverly Hills, Sage Publications, 1978).

G. el-Rashidi, *The Arabs and the World of the Seventies* (New Delhi, Vikas Publishing House, 1977).

B. Erickson, *International Networks: The Structured Webs of Diplomacy and Trade* (Beverly Hills, Sage Professional Papers in International Studies, Vol. 3, Series No. 02-037, 1975).

Ph. P. Everts, *The European Community in the World: The External Relations of the Enlarged European Community* (Rotterdam, Rotterdam University Press, 1972).

W. J. Feld, *The European Community in World Affairs: Economic Power and Political Influence* (Port Washington, New York, Alfred Publishing Co., 1976).

B. S. Frey, *Modern Political Economy* (New York, John Wiley and Sons, 1978).

C. Furtado, *Economic Development of Latin America, Historical Background and Contemporary Problems* (Cambridge, Cambridge University Press, 1976).

J. Galtung, *The European Community: A Superpower in the Making* (Oslo, Universitets Forlaget; London, George Allen & Unwin, 1973).

J. Galtung, *The True Worlds: A Transnational Perspective* (New York, The Free Press, 1980).

C. Gasteyger *et al., Europe and the Mahgreb* (Paris, Atlantic Papers No. 1, The Atlantic Institute, 1972).

K. Goldman and G. Sjostedt (eds), *Power, Capabilities, and Interdependence: Problems in the Sudy of International Influence* (Beverly Hills, Sage Publications, 1979).

A. Grotewold, *The Regional Theory of World Trade* (Grove City, Pa., Ptolemy Press, 1979).

M. T. Gunaimi, *Nadrah fi al-seasat al-Arabiyah al-Dawliah* [Theories of Arab International Relations] (Alexandria, Egypt, Al-Maarif, n.d., in Arabic).

E. B. Haas, *The Uniting of Europe: Political, Social, and Economic Forces, 1950-1958* (Stanford, Stanford University Press, 1958).

R. D. Hansen, *Beyond the North-South Stalemate, 1980 Project Council on Foreign Relations* (New York, McGraw-Hill, 1979).

J. M. Healey, *The Economics of Aid* (Beverly Hills, Sage Publications, 1971).

C. Hadlai Hull *et al., SPSS Update, New Procedures and Facilities for Releases Seven and Eight* (New York, McGraw-Hill, 1979).

International Monetary Fund, *Direction of Trade Statistics Annual* (Washington DC, IMF, issues 1961-80).

G. Ionescu (ed.), *The European Alternatives, an Inquiry into the Policies of the European Community* (The Netherlands, Alphen van den Rijn, 1979).

H. K. Jacobson, *Networks of Interdependence, International Organizations and the Global Political System* (New York, Alfred Knopf, 1979).

E. Kaufman, *The Super Powers and Their Sphere of Influence* (New York, St. Martins Press, 1976).

N. Kappagoda, *The Cost of Foreign Aid to Developing Countries* (Ottawa, Canada, International Development Research Centre, 1978).

R. Keohane and J. Nye (jun.) (eds), *Transnational Relations and World Politics* (Cambridge, Mass., Harvard University Press, 1971).

R. Keohane and J. Nye, *Power and Interdependence, World Politics in Transition* (Boston, Little, Brown, and Co., 1977).

U. Kitzinger, *Europe's Wider Horizons* (London, Federal Trust, 1975).

D. Lambert, 'Patterns of Transnational Relations', in W. Feld and G. Boyd (eds), *Comparative Regional Systems, West and East Europe, North America, the Middle East and Developing Countries* (New York, Pergamon Press, 1980).

E. Laszlo and J. Kurtzman (eds), *Western Europe and the New International Economic Order, Representative Samples of European perspectives* (New York, Pergamon Press for UNITAR, 1980).

V. Levine and W. Luke, *The Arab–African Connection: Political and Economic Realities* (Boulder, Colo., Westview Press, 1979).

R. W. Macdonald, *The League of Arab States, A Study on the Dynamics of Regional Organizations* (Princeton, Princeton University Press, 1965).

V. A. Mahler, *Dependency Approaches to International Political Economy, A Cross-National Study* (New York, Columbia University Press, 1980).

P. Maillet, *The Construction of a European Community* (New York, Praeger, 1975).

J. Matar and Ali-Din Hilal, *Arab Regional Systems, A Study in Intra-Arab Political Systems* (Beirut, Centre for Studies on Arab Unity, 1978, in Arabic).

J. D. Matthews, *Association System of the European Community* (New York, Praeger, 1977).

H. Maull, *Europe and World Energy* (London, Butterworths, 1980).

M. F. Mellah, *L'Association du Maroc à la Communauté Economique Européene, Aspects Politique* (Casablanca, Les Editions Mahgrebines, 1974).

D. C. Miller, *Handbook of Research Design and Social Measurement* (3rd edn, New York and London, Longman, 1978).

R. Morgan, *High Politics, Low Politics. Toward a Foreign Policy for Western Europe* (The Washington Papers, Vol. I, No. II, Beverly Hills and London, Sage Publications, 1973).

A. Morgon, *From Summit to Council: Evolution in the EEC* (London, Chatham House, 1976).

E. Morse, 'Crisis Diplomacy, Interdependence, and the Politics of International Economic Relations', in R. Tanter and R. Ullman (eds), *Theory and Policy in International Relations* (Princeton, Princeton University Press, 1972).

Sir H. Nicolson, *Diplomacy* (5th edn, New York, Oxford University Press, 1964).

N. Nie *et al., Statistical Package for the Social Sciences (SPSS)* (2nd edn, New York, McGraw Hill, 1975).

Organization of Economic Co-operation and Development, Development Assistance Committee, *Development Cooperation* (Paris, OECD-DAC, annual reviews).

D. Palumbo, *Statistics in Political and Behavioral Science* (New York, Columbia University Press, 1977).

W. B. Quandt, *Decade of Decisions, American Policy Toward the Arab-Israeli Conflict* (Berkeley, University of California Press, 1977).

H. H. Rasheed, *The League of Arab States* (Tunis, Seras Publications, 1980, in Arabic).

R. Rhodes (ed.), *Imperialism and Underdevelopment, A Reader* (New York, Monthly Review Press, 1970).

N. R. Richardson, *Foreign Policy and Economic Dependence* (Austin, University of Texas Press, 1978).

G. G. Rosenthal, *The Men Behind the Decisions, Cases in European Policy-Making* (Lexington, Mass., 1975).

B. Russet *et al., World Handbook of Political and Social Indicators* (2nd edn, Westport, Conn., Greenwood Press, 1977).

T. Scharf (ed.), *Trilateral Cooperation* (2 vols, Paris, OECD Development Centre Studies, 1978).

J. E. Spero, *The Politics of International Economic Relations* (New York, St. Martin's Press, 1977).

M. Sullivan, *International Relations: Theories and Evidence* (Englewood Cliffs, New Jersey, Prentice Hall, 1976).

P. Taylor and A. J. R. Groom (eds), *International Organization, A Conceptual Approach* (London, Frances Pinter, 1978).

P. Taylor, *When Europe Speaks with One Voice, the External Relations of the European Community* (Westport, Conn., Greenwood Press, 1979).

E. Volker (ed.), *Euro-Arab Cooperation* (Leyden, A. W. Sijthoff, 1976).

F. von Geusau and A. M. Alting, *Beyond the European Community* (2nd edn, Leyden, A. W. Sijthoff, 1974).

II. Documents

A. al-Hamad, director-general of the KFAED, *Some Aspects of the Kuwaiti Fund's Approach to International Development Finance* (Kuwait, Kuwaiti Fund for Arab Economic Development, December 1977).

Arab Bank for Economic Development in Africa, *Principles Governing the Bank's Policy on the Financing of Development Projects in Africa* (Khartoum, Sudan, n.d.).

Association Parlementaire pour la Coopération Euro-Arabe, *Joint Parliamentary Conference for Euro-Arab Cooperation* 'Final Declaration by the General Committee', Luxembourg, 2 July 1977.

Ibid., 'Final Cultural Report'.

Ibid., 'Joint Report of the Economic Committee'.

Commission of the European Communities, Spokesman Group and Directorate-General for Information, 'EEC-Egypt Cooperation Agreement', *Europe Information Development* (Brussels, May 1978).

Commission of the European Communities, Spokesman Group and Directorate-General for Information, 'EEC-Jordan Cooperation Agreement', *Europe Information Development* (Brussels, December 1978).

Commission of the European Communities, Directorate-General for Development, *The European Community and Changes in the International Division of Labor* (Report of an expert group on the reciprocal implications of the internal and external policies of the community, Brussels, January 1979).

Commission of the European Communities, Directorate-General for Information, 'Sudan-EEC Relations', *Europe Information Development* (Brussels, April 1979).

Commission of the European Communities, Directorate-General for and Financial Affairs, *European Economy, Annual Economic Report 1979-80*, No. 4 (Brussels, November 1979).

Commission of the European Communities, Spokesman Group and Directorate-General for Information, 'EEC-Morocco Cooperation Agreement'. *Europe Information Development* (Brussels, February 1980).

Commission of the European Communities, Spokesman Group and Directorate-General for Information, 'EEC-Syria Cooperation Agreement', *Europe Information Development* (Brussels, May 1980).

Commission of the European Communities, Spokesman Group and Directorate-General for Information, 'EEC-Lebanon Cooperation Agreement', *Europe Information Development* (Brussels, May 1980).

Commission of the European Communities, Spokesman Group and Directorate-General for Information, 'The EEC-Israel Cooperation Agreement', *Europe Information Development* (Brussels, May 1980).

Commission of the European Communities, Spokesman Group and Directorate-General for Information, 'EEC-Algeria Cooperation Agreement', *Europe Information Development* (X/123/80, Brussels, June 1980).

Commission of the European Communities, Spokesman Group, Community-Arab Funds Cofinancing' (press release, Brussels, 18 June 1980).

Commission of the European Communities, 'The Development of Trade Between the European Community and the Arab League Countries', *Europe Information Development* (X/278/80-EN, Brussels, September 1980).

Commission of the European Communities, Directorate-General for Development, *Community Involvement in Cofinancing* (Brussels, 11 November 1980).

Commission of the European Communities, Directorate-General for Economic and Financial Affairs, *European Economy*, No. 8 (Brussels, March 1981).

Dialogue Euro-Arabe, Commission General, 'Communiqué Final', Brussels, 26-8 October 1977.

Euro-Arab Dialogue, 'Joint Memorandum', Cairo, 14 June 1975 (Brussels, Commission of the European Communities).

Euro-Arab Dialogue and Commission of the European Communities, 'Joint Working Paper', Rome, 24 July 1975, (Brussels, Commission of the European Communities).

Euro-Arab Dialogue and League of Arab States, 'Joint Working Paper', Abu Dhabi, 27 November 1975 (Cairo, League of Arab States).

Euro-Arab Dialogue, General Committee, 'Joint Working Paper', Luxembourg, 18-20 May 1976 (Brussels, Commission of the European Communities, 2 June 1976).

Euro-Arab Dialogue, General Committee, 'Final Communiqué', Tunis, 10-12 February 1977 (Cairo, League of Arab States).

Euro-Arab Dialogue, General Committee, 'Final Communiqué', Brussels, 26-8 October 1977 (Brussels, Commission of the European Communities).

Euro-Arab Dialogue, General Committee, 'Final Communiqué', Damascus, 9-11 December 1978 (Cairo, League of Arab States).

Euro-Arab Dialogue, 'Meeting at the Political Level', Luxembourg, 12-13 November 1980 (Brussels, Commission of the European Communities).

European Community, 'Second Report on European Political Cooperation on Foreign Policy', *Bulletin of the European Communities*, 6/9 (1975), 12-21.

European Community, Directorate-General for Development, *Summary of Cofinanced Projects in the Context of the Financial and Technical Aid to non-Associated Developing Countries* (Brussels, September 1980).

European Community Commission, *The European Community and the Third World* (Brussels, November 1977).

European Communities, European Parliament, 'Report Drawn up on Behalf of the Committee on Agriculture on the Effects of the Mediterranean Policy on Community Agriculture', *Working Documents 1977-1978* (Document 467-77, 11 January 1978).

European Communities, European Parliament, 'Motion for a Resolution

Tabled by Mrs. Charzat, Mrs. Roudy, Mr. Sarre and Mr. Loo Pursuant to Rule 25 of the Rules of Procedure on the Situation in the Middle East', *Working Documents 1980-1981* (Document 1-101/80, Luxembourg, 16 April, 1980).

European Council, 'Declaration of the European Council on the Middle East', Venice, 12-13 June 1980 (released by the EC Information Office, Washington DC.).

European Investment Bank, *Twenty Years, 1958-1978* (Brussels, 1979).

Eurostat: Monthly External Trade Bulletin, 1958-1979 (Paris, OECD-DAC, 1980).

Kuwait: Fund for Arab Economic Development, *Cooperation with Consulting Firms* (Kuwait, February 1977).

L'Ambassade du Tunisie au Caire, *The Euro-Arab Dialogue, First General Committee Meeting, Luxembourg, 18-20 May 1976* (Cairo, 1976).

League of Arab States, 'Arab Position Paper for the Fourth Meeting of the Euro-Arab Dialogue' (Tunis, 1979, mimeographed).

League of Arab States, Secretariat-General, Euro-Arab Dialogue Unit, 'Ejtimaa al-Janib al-Arabi Fi al-Lujnah al-Aamah Lil Hiwar al-Arabi al-Urobbi' [A Meeting of the Arab Side in the EAD] (Tunis, 2 February 1980, in Arabic).

League of Arab States, Secretariat-General, 'Taqrir Lujnat al-Tafkir bil Hiwar al-Arabi al-Urrobi' [Report of the Ad-Hoc Committee on Re-establishing the Euro-Arab Dialogue] (Tunis, 2 February 1980, in Arabic).

League of Arab States, Secretariat-General, Euro-Arab Dialogue Unit, memorandum on the League's General Council decision at its seventy-second meeting, and the tenth Arab summit meeting on the EAD, 25 February 1980.

League of Arab States, Secretariat-General, 'Report to the League General Council Meeting' (report given to the seventy-fourth meeting of the General Council, held on the subject of the Euro-Arab Dialogue negotiations, Tunis, 2 September 1980).

League of Arab States, General Council, 'The League Council Decisions on the EAD in its 73rd and 84th Meetings', Tunis, 16 September 1980.

League of Arab States, Euro-Arab Dialogue Unit, 'A Report on the EAD Preparatory Meeting Held in Tunis, October 18, 1980' (Tunis, 19 October 1980).

League of Arab States, Secretariat-General, Department of Economic Affairs, 'Draft Agreement between Member Countries of the League of Arab States and Member Countries of the European Economic Community on the Mutual Promotion and Protection of Respective Investments' (Tunis, 1980).

Organization for Economic Co-operation and Development, *Geographic Distribution of Financial Flows to Developing Countries* (Paris, OECD-DAC, 1964, 1965, 1967, 1969, 1974, 1978, and 1980).

Organization of Arab Petroleum Exporting Countries, Institut Français du Petrole, *Opportunities for Cooperation between France and the Arab World* (proceedings of a joint seminar held at Versailles 4–5 November 1975, Paris, Imprimeur, 1975).

Organization of Arab Petroleum Exporting Countries, Secretary-General, Annual Report (Kuwait, OAPEC, 1974, 1975, and 1976).

Press and Information Office, Federal Republic of Germany, *Texts Relating to the European Political Cooperation* (Bonn, 1977).

R. Taylor, 'Implications for the Southern Mediterranean Countries of the Second Enlargement of the European Community' (a report to the EC Commission), *Europe Information Development* (X/225/80-EN, Brussels, June 1980).

E. Wallerstein, 'Twenty-five Years of European Community External Relations', *European Documentation* (journal of the European Community, Brussels) (April 1979).

United Nations, *Statistical Yearbook* (New York, UN, issues 1974–8).

United States Senate, Ninety-Fourth Congress, First Session, Foreign Investment Legislation, *Hearings before the Subcommittee on Foreign Commerce and Tourism of the Committee on Commerce* (Washington DC, US Government Printing Office, 1975).

III. Articles

A. S. al-Dajani, 'The PLO and the Euro–Arab Dialogue', *Journal of Palestine Studies*, 9 (Spring 1980), 81–98.

K. Abdul-Rehman al-Douri, 'An Analysis of the Euro–Arab Dialogue', *The Iraqui Economist*, 8/88, 37–43.

J. Bourrinet, 'L'Enjeau Economique du Dialogue Euro–Arabe: La Recherche d'un Accord Intercommunautaire de Development', *Annuaire de Tiers Monde*, 3 (1976–7).

J. Caporaso, 'Dependence, Dependency, and Power in the Global System: A Structural and Behavioral Analysis', *International Organization*, 30 (Winter 1978), 13–42.

E. Danignon, 'International Energy Markets', *Chemical Industry* (December 1979), pp. 812–14.

M. Dolan and J. Caporaso, 'The External Relations of the European Community', *Annals of the American Academy of Political and Social Science*, 440 (November 1978), 135–55.

T. Dos Santos, 'The Structure of Interdependence', *The American Economic Review, Papers and Proceedings*, 60 (May 1970), 231–6.

A. H. el-Mouafi, 'L'Action Commune Arabe', *Mahgrib–Machrek, La Documentation Française*, 85 (July–September 1979), 446–54.

L. S. Finkelstein, 'The IR of IGOs' (paper delivered at the annual meeting of the International Studies Association, Los Angeles, 19 March 1980).

J. Galtung, 'A Structural Theory of Imperialism', *Journal of Peace Research*, 2 (1971), 81-171.

G. S. Goodwin, 'A European Community Foreign Policy', *Journal of Common Market Studies*, 12 (September 1973), 7-27.

E. B. Haas, 'Why Collaborate? Issue-Linkage and International Regimes', *World Politics*, 32 (April 1980), 357-405.

A. Inkeles, 'The Emerging Social Structure of the World', *World Politics*, 25 (September 1973), 467-95.

R. Jenkins, 'Europe and the Third World, The Political Economy of Interdependence', *Round Table*, 272 (October 1978), 304-14.

K. Kaiser, 'The Interaction of Regional Subsystems, Some Preliminary Notes on Recurrent Patterns and the Role of Superpowers', *World Politics*, 21 (October 1968), 84-107.

M. Khouja, 'Some Observations on the Flow of Financial Resources to Developing Countries', *OAPEC Bulletin*, 6/3 (March 1980), pp. 9-15.

J. Kristiansen, 'special Report, The Arabs and Europe', *Arab Report* (31 January 1979), pp. 7-9.

R. Little and R. D. McKinlay, 'Linkage-Responsiveness and the Modern State: An Alternative View of Interdependence', *British Journal of International Studies*, 4 (1978), 209-25.

R. McGeehan, 'A Foreign Policy for the Nine?', *European Community*, Washington DC, 161 (December 1972), pp. 10-11.

R. McGeehan and S. Warneke, 'Europe's Foreign Policies: Economics, Politics, or Both?', *Orbis* (Winter 1974), 1251-79.

G. P. Papa, 'A Global Policy for the Mediterranean', *European Community*, Washington DC, 161 (December 1972), p. 12.

C. Pentland, 'The Regionalization of World Politics: Concepts and Evidence', *International Journal*, 30 (Autumn 1975), 599-630.

E. Raad, 'Al-Muatamar Athalith lil Ahzab el-Taqadumiyah wal-Ishtirakiah fi Hawidh al-Bahr al-Abiedh al-Mutawassitt' [The Third Conference of the Socialist and Progressive Parties of the Mediterranean Basin] *Al-Taliah*, Kuwait, 611 (12 June 1979), pp. 44-7, in Arabic).

L. Rainer, 'Le Dialogue Euro-Arabe et sa Place dans la Politique Méditerranéen des Neuf', *Revue du Marché Commun*, 193 (February 1976), pp. 71-3.

J. G. Ruggie, 'Collective Goods and Future International Collaboration', *American Political Science Review*, 66 (September 1972), 874-93.

T. M. Shaw, 'EEC-ACP Interactions and Images as Redefinitions of Eurofrica: Exemplary, Exclusive and/or Exploitative?', *Journal of Common Market Studies*, 28 (December 1979), 135-58.

H. Sicherman, 'Politics of Dependence: Western Europe and the Arab-Israeli Conflict', *Orbis*, 23/4 (Winter 1980), 845-57.

U. Steinbach, 'The Peace Treaty—New Era in the Middle East', *Aussen Politik* (English edn), 30 (April 1979), pp. 426-41.

W. R. Thompson, 'The Regional Subsystem, A Conceptual Explanation and a Propositional Inventory', *International Studies Quarterly,* 17 (March 1973), 89–117.

S. Yasein, 'The Politics of the Euro-Arab Journalist Dialogue' (paper presented at the Euro-Arab Journalist Dialogue, Baghdad, 26–9 January 1980).

O. Young, 'International Regimes: Problems of Concept Formation', *World Politics,* 32 (April 1980), 331–56.

IV. Miscellaneous

'Aid Extended by Third World Development Banks and Funds During Third Quarter 1979', *OAPEC Bulletin,* 6/1 (January 1980), pp. 10–11.

'Aid Extended by Third World Development Banks and Funds in 1979', *OAPEC Bulletin,* 6/2 (February 1980), pp. 10–11.

'Aid Extended by Third World Development Banks and Funds—First Quarter 1980', *OAPEC Bulletin,* 6/6 (June 1980), pp. 12–17.

'An Evaluation of OPEC Aid to LDCs, A Document', *OPEC Review,* 3/2 (Summer 1979), 1–24.

'Arab Aid to Africa: The Arab Bank for Economic Development in Africa and the Arab Fund for Technical Assistance to African and Arab Countries', *OAPEC Bulletin,* 4/7 (July 1978), pp. 22–6.

'Expansion of Activities of the Saudi Development Fund', *OAPEC Bulletin,* 4/4 (April 1978), pp. 19–23.

'Iraqi Aid Totals 3.2% of GNP', *OAPEC Bulletin,* 7/1 (January 1981), pp. 14–19.

'Islamic Development Bank (IDB) Lending Activities—a 73% Increase in 1979', *OAPEC Bulletin,* 6/5 (May 1980), pp. 8–9.

'Les Echanges Commerciaux CEE—Monde Arabe de 1979 à 1978', *Akhbar Arabia Ourobya* (special edn, 1980).

'Report: The Arab Fund for Economic and Social Development', *OAPEC Bulletin,* 4/2 (February 1978), pp. 17–23.

'The Islamic Development Bank', *OAPEC Bulletin,* 4/6 (June 1978), pp. 16–21.

'The Kuwaiti Fund for Arab Economic Development, Highlights of the Year: July 1, 1976–June 30, 1977', *OAPEC Bulletin,* 4/3 (March 1978), pp. 17–19.

'The OPEC Fund for International Development Survey of Activities 1980', *OAPEC Bulletin,* 7/4 (April 1981), pp. 20–25.

INDEX